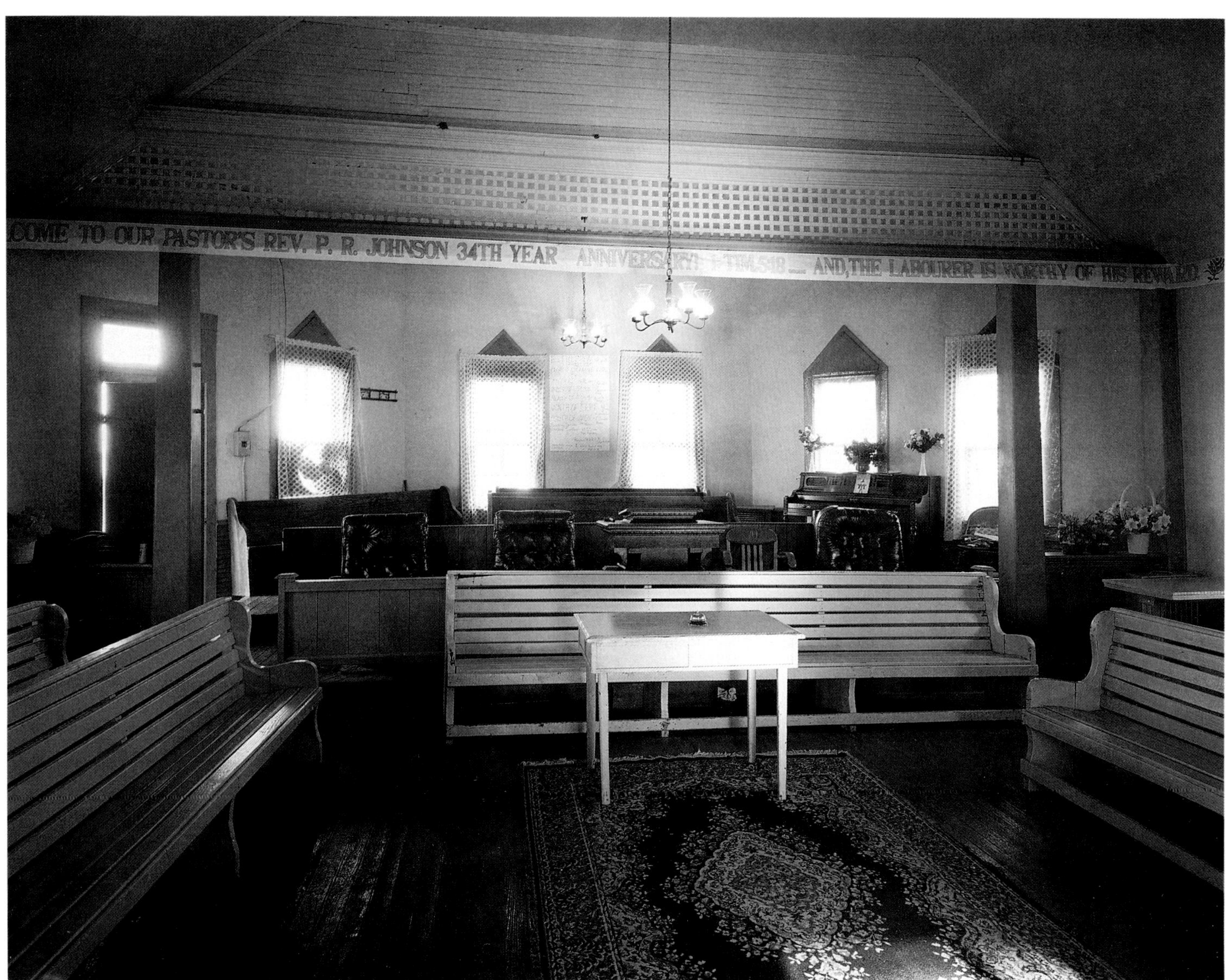
COME TO OUR PASTOR'S REV. P. R. JOHNSON 34TH YEAR ANNIVERSARY! I TIM.5:18 ... AND,THE LABOURER IS WORTHY OF HIS REWARD.

Sacred Space

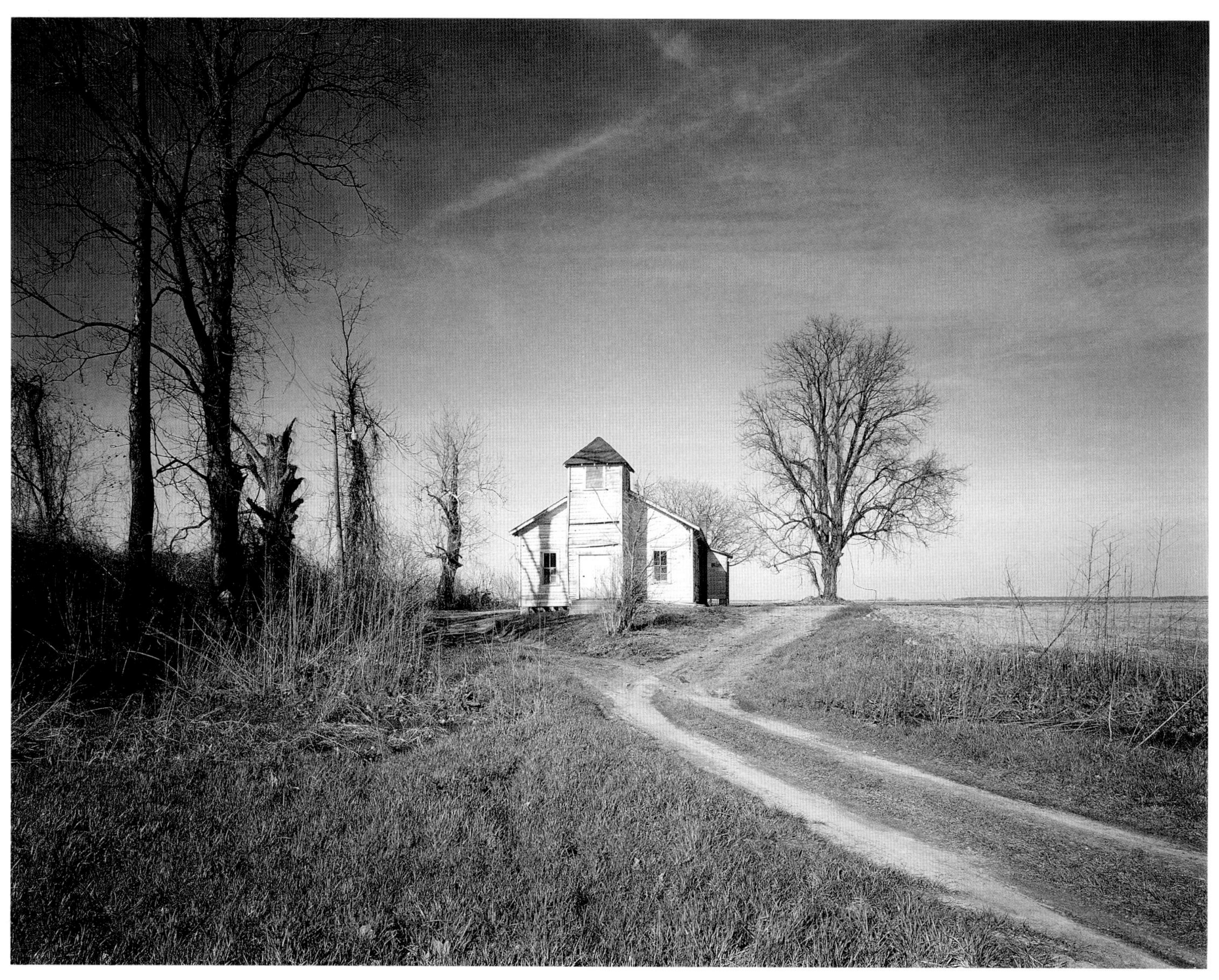

TOM RANKIN

Photographs from the Mississippi Delta

Foreword by Charles Reagan Wilson

University Press

of Mississippi

Jackson

FOR RUTHIE

Publication of this book
has been made possible in part
by a grant from
Delta State University.

Manufactured in Japan
96 95 94 93 4 3 2 1

Designed by
John A. Langston

Photographs on preceding pages:
Near Litton, 1991
Bethlehem No. 2 M. B. Church, Shaw, 1992
Mt. Tinna M. B. Church, Scott, 1990

Library of Congress Cataloging-in-Publication Data

Rankin, Tom.
Sacred space : photographs from the Mississippi Delta / by Tom Rankin ; essay by Charles Reagan Wilson.
p. cm.
ISBN 0-87805-640-8 (hard).– ISBN 0-87805-641-6 (pbk.)
1. Afro-Americans—Mississippi—Delta (Region)—Religion—Pictorial works. 2. Afro-American churches—Mississippi—Delta (Region)—Pictorial works. 3. Sacred space—Mississippi—Delta (Region)—Pictorial works. 4. Delta (Miss. : Region)—Pictorial works. I. Title.
BR563.N4R29 1993
277.62′40828′0896073—dc20 93-6973
CIP

British Library Cataloging-in-Publication data available

Foreword

by Charles Reagan Wilson

Tom Rankin's photographs chart the spiritual geography of African-Americans in the Mississippi Delta. For the ancient Greeks, the unseen presences in a place determined its nature as sacred or profane. Rankin's images are haunted by palpable if hidden signs of the spirituality of a people in a distinct time and place.

The black Delta Christians captured in these photographs are linked to other African-American worshippers through a long tradition. Before the Civil War, blacks in the South generally worshipped in biracial churches, mostly Baptist and Methodist. They took part in the First and Second Great Awakenings in the eighteenth and early nineteenth centuries and later in summer revivals, drawing from European church traditions in the process but also influencing the shape and content of the evangelicalism that would come to dominate the South. The "invisible institution" was the religion of the slave quarters, a secret religion practiced in the woods or away from the masters' attention. Here God did not sanction slavery but condemned it. The new children of bondage waited, trusting in the Divine for their liberation. The praise house was the setting and shouting was the ritual that marked this religion as distinctive, the worshippers drawing on an African heritage of danced religion.

Emancipation enabled freed slaves to withdraw from white-dominated biracial churches and to form their own separate congregations and denominations. The National Baptist Convention came to be the umbrella group representing many local, mostly independent churches. The African Methodist Episcopal church, the African Methodist Episcopal Zion church, the Colored (later Christian) Methodist Episcopal church, spin-offs from the National Baptists, and later Holiness and Pentecostal groups all organized African-American religious impulses into enduring institutions represented in the Mississippi Delta.

Under slavery and later under Jim Crow segregation, the church became central to black group identity. It was a social center, a locus for protest against racial discrimination, and a training-ground for leaders in the black community. It also carried forward African-American cultural traditions, including storytelling, dance, and drama, and its influence on music is recognized around the world. The local church, in short, gathered together widely scattered rural blacks to form a community that could implement common objectives and maintain the culture's traditions.

The religion illustrated here is a part of that tradition. Many of the churches and graveyards in the Delta go back a century; some are older. The land was a great swampy forest then. Not until the railroad came into the Delta, along with timber workers to clear the land and federal government money to help with flood control along the Mississippi River, did large numbers of settlers appear. Among them were the freedmen, seeking opportunity on a new frontier in the South.

In the twentieth century, many African-Americans whose toil had made the Delta a wealthy place for others left because they did not share in the land's bounty. But these home churches have a powerful hold on their people, those who have gone to live elsewhere as well as those who stayed. Between 20 and 25 percent of all African-American churches are rural (a figure double the size of the black rural population), and churches in the non-metropolitan South have the highest rates of membership among all African-Americans. Many of the Delta congregations were founded in the late 1800s and early 1900s, originally housed in wooden frame buildings; these photographs show some that are still around. In other cases, groups have decided to build with brick because of its greater prestige and durability.

Many of the congregants of these churches are poor in worldly goods. It is often said that the church has been a survival mechanism for people with hard lives. Tom Rankin's photographs enable us to look more deeply into black religious life, beyond easy categorizations. Perhaps some of us have not been able to see what has always been there, because we think of black religion so much in terms of voices rather than images: the chanting preacher, the "amens" of the congregation, the sweet choirs, the distinctive piano sounds. Rankin helps to open our eyes.

These photographs of sacred spaces provide a visual metaphor for African-American religious experience. One notices first the settings. The buildings are on flat land that often stretches toward the horizon. The environment is lush, with shrubs, bushes, vines, and weeds all around. The church grounds are often adjacent to a cottonfield: in the distance is the daily work area of the people who worship here. One picture shows cotton growing almost to the church door. Churches and graveyards cling to a small territory, indicating their vulnerability to the profane world. This is God's acre, but it is not always at ease.

These spaces assert the division of the sacred from the profane. Sacred phenomena are separate from daily, ordinary life, from the commonplace. Religion is intentional: people make clear by naming and by practice what is sacred, and maintaining these boundaries is a function of all religion. The spaces illuminated in these photographs are set aside for a purpose beyond work, beyond the daily harshness and injustice known by generations of black people in the Delta.

Natural features of the landscape often take on religious meaning, as an entryway to the divine. Trees—cypresses, great oaks, and others—are especially important religious symbols here. Vertical objects, like the branches of these Delta trees reaching heavenward, represent the intersection of the spiritual and human worlds. Other natural forms as well as trees create shadows that haunt these landscapes. Rankin's photographs are filled with the interplay of light and dark.

Inside the churches, the small spaces and low ceilings create an especially intimate setting for contact with the Divine. The interiors suggest a fundamental appeal of the holy: orderliness. They are places of purity, with none of the messiness of the profane world. The enclosed space is clearly divided into levels: the congregation is separated from the pulpit and choir and piano. Yet the space is so small that the congregation and those involved in conducting the worship service can interact freely, so that it is easy to imagine the lines between them dissolving.

The iconography is striking: Leonardo da Vinci's *Last Supper* hangs from a wall; nearby is a Church Covenant (indicating that these people are resolutely Protestant). A ceiling fan hangs from on high, and an awareness of time is indicated by a clock inside a bell and by a calendar. Jesus is the key figure. Crosses suggest his sacrifice and, surprisingly, even a crucifix hangs starkly on a panelled wall. He is especially prominent on painted windows, which suggest stained glass. My favorite is the church where Jesus is painted on four windows; the fourth window also holds an air-conditioner, creating a bifurcated Jesus.

These interiors, true sanctuaries, are miniature celestial cities offering vivid images of hope.

If churches are often situated so that light plays off them, suggesting illumination, graveyards are places of darkness. Sometimes overtaken with scrub brush and weeds, mostly they are scraped clean, all contaminants gone. Thrusting up out of these burial places are imaginative grave markers: homemade angels with wings, carved in the solidity of concrete. The cemeteries are usually located under prominent trees, resulting in a dark and sometimes forbidding atmosphere that suggests the fear and dread humans often bring to encounters with the sacred.

The holy in most religious traditions evokes dread and awe. Ghosts could indeed be about, reminders of the history of this land, of the suffering borne by its black inhabitants. But these burial sites are also cool and refreshing in the Mississippi climate, places of refuge, offering welcome relief from the scalding summer sun.

The cemeteries show the boundaries between the sacred and the profane. Clumps of bushes along the edges roughly but clearly demarcate these sacred spaces. Medieval European walls were military fortifications, but they began as magical protection lines against the forces of chaos embodied in demons beyond the enclosure. Past the lines of bushes here lie the cottonfields. Sometimes that land is literally dead, a wasteland created by poisonous chemical sprayings. It is close geographically but spiritually well removed.

Rituals sanctify a sacred space. Salvation is a central part of the predominant religion of the Delta, and conversion and initiation are fraught with meaning. The baptism ritual embodies the essence of the faith, and the people in these photographs of river baptisms are pilgrims, black-clad holy men and white-clad holy women standing in water, seeking sanctification. It is a timeless scene, these holiness people marching off as to glory, to a ceremony recharging a people's faith.

As we look at these places and people, they seem quiet and peaceful and calm. That is one dimension of the holy. Another is the power of exaltation. Contact with the Divine results in urgent, compelling, and spontaneous energy. Religion infuses its black followers with energy, this emotional power.

In studying the cultural significance of African-American religion, we often do not look closely enough at the sources of its power. Rankin helps us to understand those sources. The sacred can be disturbingly paradoxical: gentle, nurturing, and serene for believers, yet also violent and unpredictable. These sacred spaces in the Mississippi Delta have indeed nurtured tranquility for suffering souls; they have also been the source of a divine energizing. Power carries with it the possibility of renewal and freedom, ideas that have long driven African-American spirituality. Now we can see what it has meant to people who have lived through hard times to maintain sacred spaces such as these.

The ceremonies of African-American spirituality depicted here do not provide merely cathartic release; they represent the opportunity for transcendence. Each new initiate renews the group and its fellowship with God. Access to the Divine leads to the hope of perfection in earthly lives.

African-American churches in the Mississippi Delta are much more than social and service centers for the community, important as those functions are. Profound mysteries are at work here; lives can be transformed, hope given for the future.

These sacred places represent the transition between the world of the invisible institution of slave times and the modern black church. They are holy relics of the traditional world of an older South. Many of the churches seen here no longer exist; at least one of the preachers has passed away. Tom Rankin's photographs are sensitive renderings of a world of primordial attachments, full of fears and joys and expectations.

On Praying Ground

by Tom Rankin

The landscape of the Mississippi Delta—flat, fertile, and watery—is both vast and intimate. Over a century of intense plantation agriculture has bred a complex social order rooted in the agrarian experience, defined by a powerful sense of indigenous traditions, and ever cognizant of its history of racial tension and struggle. No single institution in the Delta region has had a more profound impact on the entire culture of the Mississippi Delta than the countless African-American churches that accent the landscape. The ubiquitous presence of these churches and their adjoining cemeteries and churchyards—these sacred spaces—constitutes a kind of three-dimensional iconography in an otherwise profane agricultural landscape. Landmarks to some, places of spiritual refuge to others, "home church" to their devoted members, these centers of religious and social life have been planned, built, decorated, and maintained by local communities for heartfelt reasons. Religious historian C. Eric Lincoln has written that the African-American experience in America was made "less onerous" because of this heartfelt, community-based religion. And the church, he says, has provided a powerful institution:

> Church was their school, their forum, their political arena, their social club, their art gallery, their conservatory of music. It was lyceum and gymnasium as well as sanctum sanctorum. Their religion was the peculiar sustaining force that gave them the strength to endure when endurance gave no promise, and the courage to be creative in the face of their own dehumanization.

Delta churches, then, continue to provide a "sustaining force" both symbolically and practically.

My photographs of sacred space within the African-American communities of the Mississippi Delta grow out of a realization of the significant role the African-American church has had in shaping the entire fabric of Delta culture. When I moved to take a teaching position at Delta State University in 1988, I began photographing the Mississippi Delta. I began to realize that the churches of the region to which I was continually drawn hold a history, an expressive culture, a landscape reflective of the peculiar place that African-Americans have held in this historically oppressive region. Perhaps no cultural window provides such a potentially meaningful view into a society as that of inherited religious traditions. I began wandering the Delta in search of expressive churches, photographing church interiors, exteriors and adjoining graveyards; attending and documenting services; and interviewing preachers. My work was constantly facilitated and enriched by the understanding and generosity of the many church members and communities I visited.

Often built by the hands of community and congregation members, these churches are designed, furnished, and embellished by them to provide a sacred context for worship and community gatherings. Thus the look and life of the church, inside and out, reflect the attitudes, beliefs, aspirations, and realities of the community. Just as stories, prayers, sermons, and songs provide a glimpse into the wisdom and power of sacred folk culture, a close look at these sacred spaces also provides rich insight.

In his book *Parting the Waters*, Taylor Branch writes that the African-American church "served not only as a place of worship but also as a bulletin board to a people who owned no organs of communication, a credit union to those without banks, and even a kind of people's court." "Black churches," argues Lincoln, "have carried burdens and performed roles and functions beyond their boundaries of spiritual nurture in politics, economics, education, music, and culture." In short, the African-American churches of the Delta, like churches throughout the South, were *the* meeting place and consequently served nearly every need of the community.

Not surprisingly, when emotions stirred to gain the right to vote in the late 1950s and 1960s, the rural African-American church was at the center of the effort. Church women, deacons, and preachers became voting rights advocates and civil rights activists, and the physical church buildings became symbols of community strength, resolve, and commitment to equality. A survey of African-American churches by C. Eric Lincoln and Lawrence H. Mamiya in 1978 revealed that between 1962 and 1965, ninety-three churches, mostly rural, were burned or bombed. Most of this violence occurred in the rural South.

One characteristic example of white violence toward churches in the Delta occurred in Issaquena County. Bruce Hilton in his 1969 book *The Delta Ministry* recounts the struggle of St. John's Missionary Baptist Church, located some eight or ten miles west of Glen Allan. According to Hilton, in 1965 the congregation of St. John's was divided over whether to use the church as a Head Start center. Some members were committed to the Head Start program. Others in the church, citing the number of churches burned throughout the South in the mid-sixties, advised against such involvement. "After all, they argued," wrote Hilton, "this church was the only thing some members could call their own. They had squeezed pennies to build it and keep it up. It was not right, they argued, to risk losing it, even for a good project." The ambivalence reflected in St. John's congregation was common throughout the region. But those in favor of the Head Start program won out. The Head Start program opened one Monday morning and sometime around 2 A.M. the following Tuesday the church caught fire and burned. Hilton recalls that some thirty feet away from the old church site "stands a new brick church. 'Fireproof,' the members tell you." To many segregationist whites, the African-American church represented a threat to the status quo, as some church members refused to remain passive and silent. While most pastors and preachers did not participate in the civil rights movement in the Delta, enough did to reinforce the image of the church and pastor as a force for racial equality. The same 1978 survey found that more than half of all African-American church congregations in the country involved themselves in some way with civil rights organizations and causes.

At the turn of the century, W. E. B. Dubois declared that "the preacher is the most unique personality developed by the Negro on American soil." One might argue the same today in the Mississippi Delta and other parts of the American South. The preacher at a rural church occupies the center of the community's religious life. A modern-day Delta preacher will often serve up to four churches, attending a different one each Sunday of the month, with the occasional fifth Sunday providing the opportunity for him either to serve as a guest preacher or to go to his home church. Churches that have services only one Sunday a month generally have Sunday school each weekend, and may also host prayer meetings on Monday or Wednesday evenings. Numerous churches are kept alive in the Delta because a strong core of members who feel attached and committed to their home church go to great lengths to ensure the continuation of worship and the preservation of the physical structure. While the casual observer might think that it would be more efficient for four congregations to join arms and support one large church, such a notion misses one of the main points of the rural black religious tradition. The church survives not only as a place of worship, but also as a symbol to the membership of a sacred home where a formal commitment to religion began, where family meets, and where forebears once gathered. A native African-American Deltan might live in Detroit, Chicago, or Memphis for over half a lifetime, but the person's funeral and burial will probably take place at his or her home church in the Mississippi Delta.

Reverend Flem Bronner, who grew up on a plantation at Perthshire, in Bolivar County, came back home from Missouri where he frequently preaches in large, urban churches in St. Louis. During a revival sermon on Perthshire Plantation, he stressed the significance of the small New Bethel Church in his life. "I've preached in some of the largest black churches in St. Louis," Reverend Bronner extolled. "Churches where eight hundred folks can sit down." He looked out intently over the seventeen faithful gathered in New Bethel, a building that might hold sixty-five with some careful arranging. "I been to big churches. I've sung in large halls. I've preached in them. But my uncle [Reverend Tom Bronner] helped bring me to Jesus right here. I was baptized across that cotton field over yonder," he said, pointing over his shoulder toward Stamps Lake. "When I hear the word 'church' I think of New Bethel. I don't care where I am, how many people in front of me. Church, to me, is this building, is New Bethel. This building. This place."

Flem Bronner's acknowledgment of the symbolic impor-

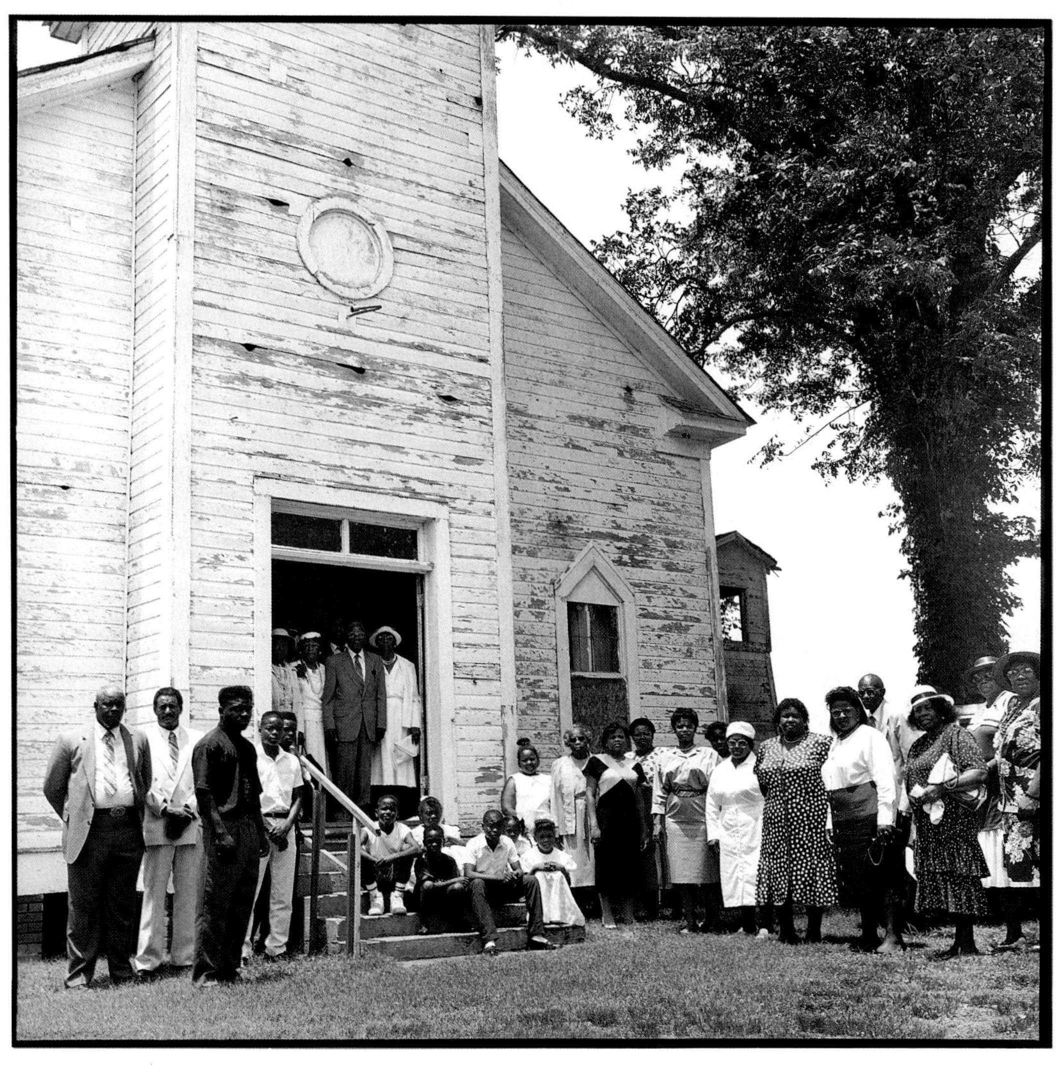

Congregation outside Bethlehem No. 2

tance of New Bethel Church was punctuated often with "amen," "yeah," and "Go on, preacher," and "Tell it, preacher." Clearly those in attendance at the church that evening, while thunder was shaking the small frame structure and lightning illuminating the many scars from decades of use and wear, understood the reverend's point. His religious life started at Perthshire and he would forever think of that place as its source. However humble and worn, it is for him a hallowed place.

Pastor P. R. Johnson, an elderly preacher in the town of Leland, once told me about the origin of one of the four churches he serves, New Prosperity Missionary Baptist Church in Arcola. While he didn't actually start New Prosperity, he was the church's first pastor and has been its only one for the past fifty-three years. New Prosperity had its name and a small congregation when Pastor Johnson attended his first Sunday school there:

> Wasn't no church. Little old house. I built the church. I was the man that built the church out there. Wasn't no church out there [then]. Wasn't a church. Folks had moved out there from Bourbon, all around Trail Lake, out there, go to buying land out there. Out there on Black Bayou. Little old two-room house. Started having Sunday school out there. Knocked that partition out and that's where they had the little wooden benches and they'd hold Sunday school.
>
> I went one Sunday. "We gonna let you preach. We gonna preach out here." So I got up behind the table there and preached. The deacons said, "That's our man right there, that's our man right there." [He laughs.] And from then on, I'm the first man that ever been out there. Preached in that house about a year and a half.

Pastor Johnson later had a church building constructed by a local lumber company, but even with that "outside" help New Prosperity was always the product of the needs and desires and motivations of its community. The church has always been shaped by the collective efforts of the hearts and hands of the entire congregation, under the leadership of the pastor, deacons, and church mothers. The church that Johnson originally built was a small, simple wood frame structure. He later modernized it and replaced part of it that had rotted; later still, he tore the old church down and built one of cinder blocks nearby. With each improvement, each addition, each new church, the congregation consulted and helped, eventually making it their own. These buildings represent the handiwork of an entire church community, forming a cooperative statement about what is appropriate for worship, what is meaningful, what is truly sacred. P. R. Johnson later became a carpenter himself and built a church from steps to steeple outside Elizabeth, near Leland. The Elizabeth church is a modern, brick-facade structure literally built by its pastor.

Theologians and educators Benjamin E. Mays and Joseph W. Nicholson argued in 1933 that one of the certain strengths of the church within the African-American community was that it was owned outright by blacks: "The church was the first community or public organization that the Negro actually owned and completely controlled. And it is possibly true to this day that the Negro church is the most thoroughly owned and controlled public institution of the race." The cultural value of this ownership continues to be important.

One pastor recounted to me the way a church was typically built in the early part of this century. He described the main builders, not surprisingly, as simply "a group of black men." He went on:

> Somebody in that crowd was a carpenter. Had him a hammer and a saw. He'd get there and go out in the woods and use them old groundhog sawmills and that's where he'd get his lumber from. From a groundhog sawmill. Cut him some cypress blocks, the church's foundation on cypress blocks. If he didn't have a sawmill, them old men could take their axes and saws, split those logs and chisel them and make them sills. They'd make them. And you'd have an old man there with a froe. He'd get out there and get him some cypress and he'd split that timber. If he wanted inch-thick timber, how wide he wanted it, he'd use his froe. Whatever you wanted. Get them those good cypress trees out there. He'd rive that stuff up. Didn't have to go to no sawmill. Sit out there in those woods and rive that timber. Had them boards straightened down then. Put battens on them.

Reverend Brooks Tobe and his wife, also a preacher, built a small church immediately across from their house and store in Rosedale. He had been a member of the Mt. Hebron Church of Rosedale for many years but was guided by God to build a new church from the bottom up. His story is typical in that he believes that his calling, his pastoral work, and the actual place of the church were directed by divine message.

Tobe and his wife acquired an old house and had it moved to a vacant lot across from

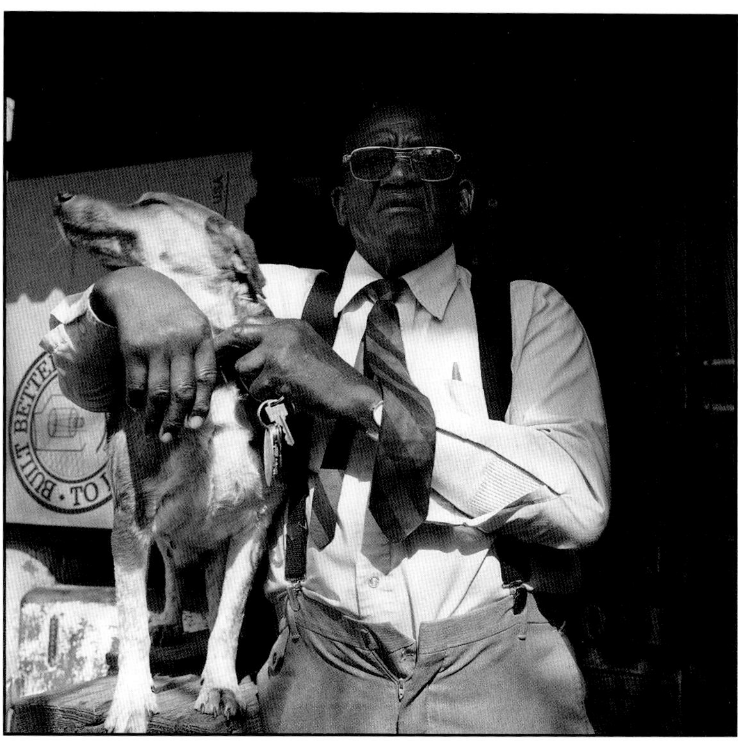

Reverend Brooks Tobe and dog at home, Rosedale, 1991

their store. Reverend Tobe remembers not knowing what to do with the building at the time:

So, after we got the building in there, got it all lined up and everything, then we began to think about a church. And I had a vision about the church. On that same block where that building set there, there's a light shined on me standing on that ground from heaven. And there's two old ladies I used to see after called Ms. Sara Lee, and that voice said, "Don't forget Sara Lee and them now." It just shined on me. I know where the spot at now. I wondered about it, said it's something or another about this ground the Lord shined a light on.

So I got to thinking about Paul was on the Damascus Road. He was going to persecute the church. When that light shined on him from heaven, it knocked him off his feet down to the ground. And a voice spoke to him, said, "Paul, why persecute, tell me?"

Said, "Who is that, Lord?"

"Get up on your feet and go straight on down the same road. There's a man down there called Ananias. He'll tell you what I have thee to do."

Reverend Tobe took the message and began to remodel the old house into a church. He had little money, but remembers that every time he found himself short of nails, siding, or other building materials someone would come by and donate money or supplies:

That didn't look like very much money, but you think about a gift somebody give you. You didn't even ask for it. I began to work on the old building and I wondered how I was gonna do that. And I began to put an extension on the front, began to make an opening for to go in. And I hadn't even got my siding for the church. So the Lord made a way for me to get some siding. A man just brought the stuff to me. And I took it and put it on that far side of yonder. Well, I began to work on the old building. I began to wonder about my nails and how I was gonna do that. And everytime I thought I was out of nails, somebody would come there and give me money to get nails. Said, I can't get out of this thing.

All this has come from somewhere, when I made up my mind that this was gonna be a church. And everytime I thought I didn't have something, God sent somebody to give me. When I thought I was too tired, overnight I would gain all my strength. And be ready to work the next day.

As Tobe believes he was sent a directive from God to build his church, he also feels the congregation consists of individuals sent by God. Many of the same people who gave him materials and money with which to build became the congregation and church community. They helped him make the structure into a church and eventually into a vital, if small, house of worship. "And on through life I saw myself building," Tobe recalls. "And He give me that whole vision and said, 'Brooks, you're gonna build all the way through there. Build on. Build my church there. Because my church is up on the rock. The very gates of hell shall not prevail it. For she's settin' on the rock over there.'"

The name for Reverend Tobe's church came to him almost as quietly and surely as his directive to build it in the first place: "It hit me in the heart—Little Ebenezer Baptist Church. It just come to me." Little Ebenezer takes as its model—at least in part—'big' Ebenezer Baptist Church in Atlanta where Martin Luther King, Jr., was pastor and is now buried.

The architecture of older Delta churches is traditional. Reverend P. R. Johnson explained the single most common element of the African-American church building:

> All of the churches had bell towers. Yeah, that's all they knowed. Wasn't no bell tower on it, wasn't no church. That's what had the bell in it. Yea, they ring that bell. Sunday mornings you could hear that bell ringing for Sunday school and when Sunday school is out you hear that bell ringing to let 'em know ready for service then. Fellow that didn't go to Sunday school he know that Sunday school is out. By hearing that bell ring. Somebody die, make it to the church, ring the bell. You know somebody was dead. Tone the bell. You know somebody was dead. Hit it a certain way. Hit it about two or three times real fast and then stop. You know somebody was dead. That's the way they did then.

The bell tower became a ubiquitous image across the landscape of the Delta. Although the old bell tower churches are slowly being replaced by more modern brick churches sporting simple steeples, the bell towers that remain are proud symbols of the past.

The same is true for other sacred places such as small church cemeteries. Churches and cemeteries on plantations were frequently placed on marginal land abutting cotton

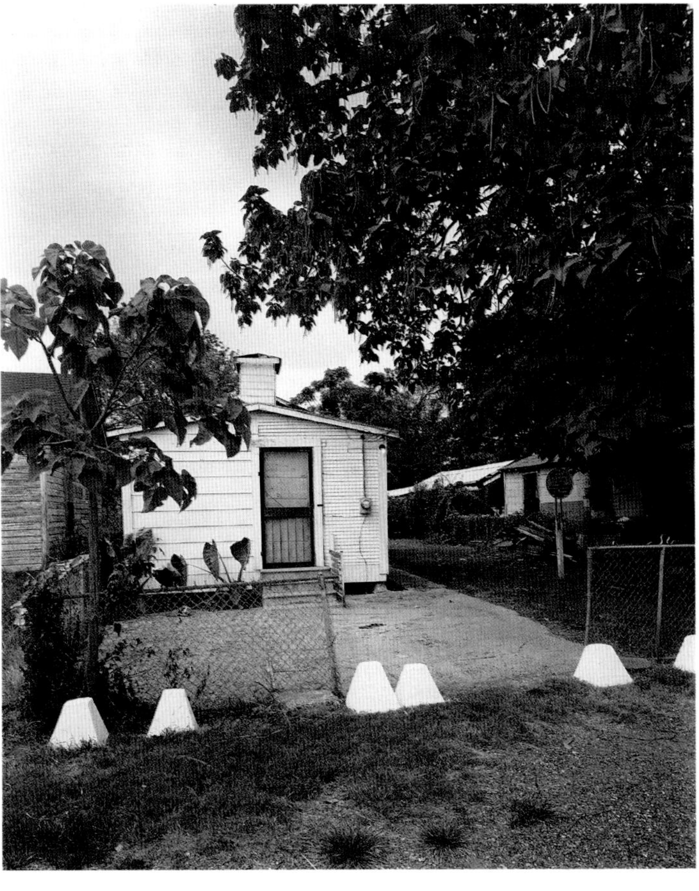

Little Ebenezer Baptist Church, Rosedale, 1990

fields, turn rows [dirt roads beside farm fields] and bayous. Cemeteries, some now over a century old, were frequently placed on low, "heavy" ground that was not suitable for growing good cotton. Today, these cemeteries, many displaying handmade gravestones as well as the more modern engraved monuments, border agricultural fields, roads, and catfish ponds. As crop lands in the Delta are regularly transformed by large John Deere tractors pulling disks, plows, cultivators, and land levelers, the postage-stamp-size cemeteries and churchyards remain relatively unscarred by the work, stoic reminders of the permanence of the church and the faith of its congregations. Church members and descendents of the buried often refer to these places as "our little cemetery," using a tone of ownership and control, just as they do when they speak of "my church."

Traditional outdoor baptisms represent perhaps the quintessential transformation of an existing place into a sacred space. Though the number of outdoor baptisms in bayous, lakes, and rivers has declined in recent years—the natural bodies of water having been supplanted by churchyard and indoor baptismal pools—some congregations are holding on to the traditional practice because of its history and the symbolic relationship with the original baptism of Jesus by John the Baptist in the River Jordan. Reverend Tom Bronner of Gunnison, for example, held firmly to the tradition of baptizing in Stamps Lake on Perthshire Plantation, the place where he himself had been baptized in his teens. He continued to take candidates for baptism to the very same spot on the lake each August until his death in 1989.

Reverend Bronner's own religious life had begun near Stamps Lake, where he had been instructed by his preacher to find "a praying ground, go to that praying ground and pray and ask God" for forgiveness. His preacher instructed him to go to his chosen place daily until the Lord spoke to him. He did that for two weeks, going to the same place "under a pecan bush on the bogue bank" [bank of a creek or stream] each day. Some sixty years later Reverend Bronner remembered that he "had been there so many times it was clean where I had been there praying, begging God to bless my soul." In his chosen sacred spot under that pecan bush he found God.

He described receiving his divine call to preach close by his old praying ground near the sharecropper's house where he lived:

I was living at Perthshire. On the bogue bank, we called it. And I was on my way home on a dirt road beside a canal ditch that led into the bogue where I lived. And I was walking, stepping. Now it didn't slip up on me, the Lord had been worrying me a long time about preaching. And I talked to God like I'm talking to you. I said, "I ain't gonna preach."

But something was within me, was, just like I'm talking to you, saying, "I mean for you to preach."

I say, "I ain't got sense enough to preach. You get after someone else. Let me do what I'm doing." [I'm] talking to God.

As I was stepping I got paralyzed. The Lord knows I'm telling you the truth. I couldn't move. I had my same mind, I had my same eyes. I could see my same person sitting on the bogue. I couldn't lift my feet. I said, "Lord." I couldn't, but I tried. While I was standing there talking back to God he was talking to me. I could hear the voice saying, "I say preach."

I said, "No, I ain't."

And I stood there arguing with God about what I wasn't going to do. It looked like I come to my sense. I said, "Well, if you let me go home, I'll preach." And my legs started walking. I walked up to the house.

I know it. There are two things I know. I know I've been converted. And I know I've been called to preach. Them two things. Ain't much I know. But those two things I'm sure of.

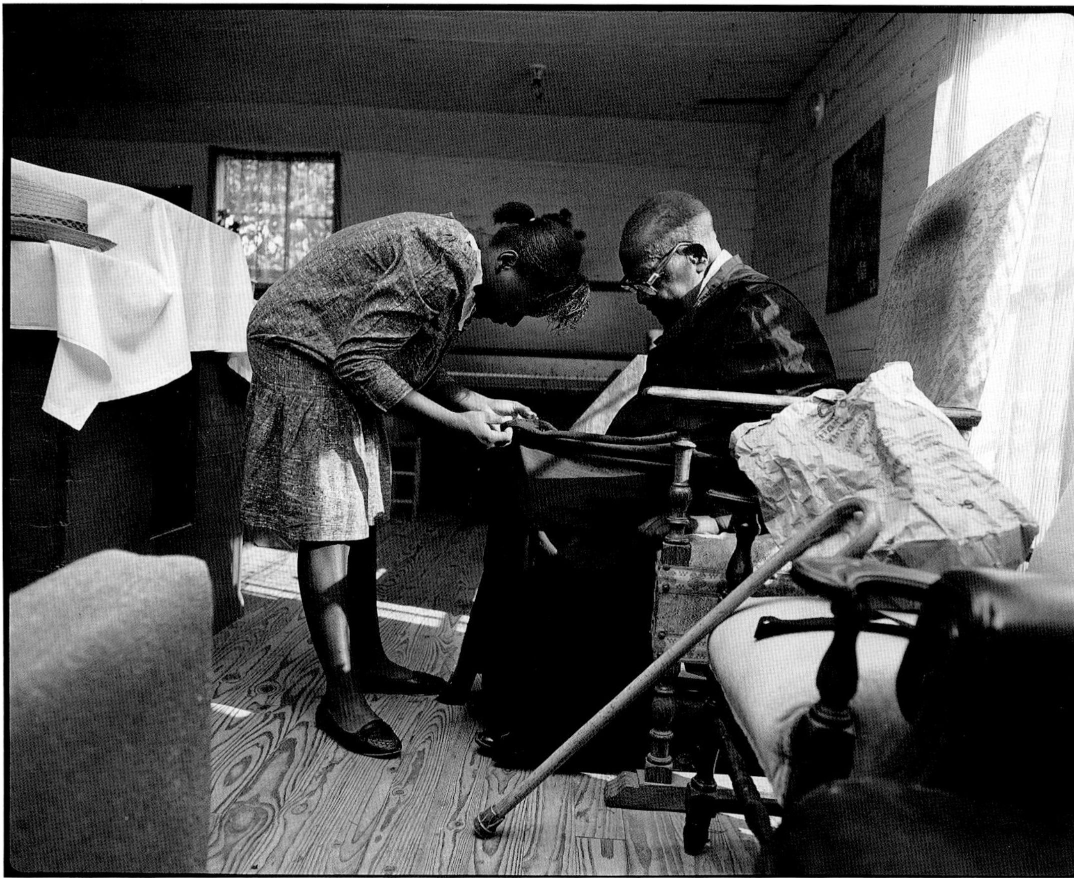

Reverend Tom Bronner and his niece, 1989

With the certainty of his calling, Reverend Bronner led the New Bethel Church at Perthshire for over fifty years. In each of those years, after the annual revival held in August because that was the traditional "lay by" time when the cotton was too tall for laborers to work so they had time off until picking season, he took his church members to Stamps Lake for the annual baptism. Large crowds gathered—many more than attended the preceding church service—to watch the time-honored outdoor ritual. As Bronner's age began to catch up with him, he could no longer walk into the water; his legs were not strong enough to withstand the uneven footing on the lake bottom. But he was not discouraged—he began inviting a guest minister to help him with the ceremony and to venture out into the water to conduct the actual submersion.

At Tom Bronner's last baptism, in 1989, he was very feeble and moved slowly with his cane, accepting a helpful hand from numerous people as he walked into the church and up to his chair behind the pulpit for the service that would precede the trip to the lake. He quoted from Scripture to his church members: "As Jesus say, 'Go in the hedges and highways and compel them to come.' But not with a gun, but with a good life. You can compel people to come to Jesus. The way is open there for anybody that is willing to be saved. Jesus said when he was here, 'He that believeth and are baptized shall be saved.' I don't believe that he was playing when he said those words. So we're going to the lake very pleased and very happy to have one to be baptized. Amen."

He explained to the congregation the importance of the annual trip to Stamps Lake—though most knew already—and then gave thanks to Reverend Tom Meek who would help him by wading in the water: "Brother Meek, one of our good pastors. We blessed to know he's a member of this church. Haven't ever had a minute's trouble. He's always been obedient. He's leaving here to go to the baptizing at his church. I think that's so sweet of him to turn aside and come help an old man who's been pastoring fifty years."

Quietly Bronner led the church in hymn:

I heard the voice of Jesus say,
I heard the voice of Jesus say,
Come unto me and rest.

The church emptied. The lake was a mile or so away on Highway 32, down a small dirt road. As people got out of their cars to walk down to the lake's edge, they began to sing slow, traditional hymns. Reverend Bronner opened with prayer, thanking God for "saving us from a burning hell" and saying, "We're here this morning, a day and place we've been coming to a many a day," an acknowledgment of the tradition of bringing candidates to this very place on Stamps Lake. As he continued with his prayer, those gathered began to sing:

Lord have mercy on a child
like me
Lord have mercy on a child
like me

Through the beautiful and deliberate sounds of the congregational singing, Bronner's prayerful voice continued, "We feel good to stand out in the world. Oh, Lord, look on us and smile." The congregation sang on:

I didn't see nobody, but I felt
the change
I didn't see nobody, but I felt
the change

Bronner closed his prayer, exhorting, "The victory is ours, take our souls home."

As the deacons, the candidate, and Reverend Meek carefully walked out into waist-deep water, one church member began leading the others in song. He would continue throughout the service to lead the singing:

Jesus keep me near the cross
There's a precious fountain
Free to all a heavenly stream
Flow from Calvary's mountain.

From that point, it was Reverend Meek's service. Standing

in the water with his hand on the baptismal candidate, Obedian, he preached a sermon with immense eloquence and power. Those gathered on the bank were attentive and responsive, encouraging him, punctuating his message, even singing in the midst of his sermon. The beauty of the music and chanted sermon resonating off the water and cypress trees in the humid August air was extraordinary. The clearing on the bank of Stamps Lake, recently mowed by a cotton planter's crew and usually occupied only by turtles or water moccasins and perhaps a lone person fishing, was transformed by the presence and power of the baptism into an outdoor cathedral.

As Reverend Meek stood in the water shoulder to shoulder with two deacons from New Bethel Church, he dipped his hands in and out of the water, creating a fluid, almost percussive background sound as he sang out his sermon and the people responded:

Every heart say amen.
[AMEN]
We're here to carry out one of the greatest commandments
When Jesus walked down to Jordan
To be baptized
He told John and John baptized me
John said, I'm not worthy to be baptizing thee
But need to be baptized by thee
Told him suffer it to be so
That we might, that we would fulfill the scriptures that was spoken of by the prophet
When straight away John led Jesus on out in Jordan
And the heaven's door was open
And the spirit descended down like the shape of a dove
And lit upon Jesus' shoulder
And I heard the voice from heaven way saying,
This is my beloved son
Whom I am well pleased.
He told us to hear, heed him
Oh and God's word is all right
I want you to know He's all right
I heard the songwriter wrote the other day,
He that believeth on the Father and the Son shall have an everlasting life.

Ephesians two and eight said, For by
Grace He saved through faith which is not by yourself
But it is a gift of God, ah
It is a gift of God
That gift is that if we believe
In the name of Jesus
I heard Peter say the other day
That there is no other name given among men
Whereby that we might be saved
And that is through the name of Jesus
Oh yeah
I wonder, can I get a witness
Wonder do you know He all right
He's all right
He's all right

[CONGREGATION SINGS: GOT RELIGION AND I'M SATISFIED
GOT RELIGION AND I'M SATISFIED]

He's all right
I know He all right
Just the other day
Just the other day
Oh, the other day
The other day
This young man came to Jesus
And that reminds me of a blind man

That was standing by the
wayside
He was blind and could not
see
He stood there and cried out,
Lord
The son of David, have mercy
On us
I heard somebody say make
'em be quiet
I heard he cried out loud
Said, Oh the son of David
have mercy on us
Oh yeah
But I heard Jesus when He
walked over to the blind
man
And asked him what would
God have me to do
I heard him, said, Oh Lord,
we want to receive our
sight
He's all right
I want you to know He's all
right
I got a message the other
day
The young man inquired
about Jesus

I heard him say, I'm lost
Been here a long time
In darkness
And I want to receive my
sight
I heard Him say that you can
believe
And be baptized, thy shall be
saved
All you to do is believe in the
name of Jesus
I heard him say if you believe
He shall have an everlasting
life
You got to first believe
Believe what?
Believe that Jesus is the Son
of God
Second, you got to repent
From your sins
Turn around, like the songwri-
ter wrote the other day
The things I used to do, I
don't do no more
Oh yes, baptism is a symbol
of Christ's death, burial
and resurrection
Oh, He's all right
Obedian

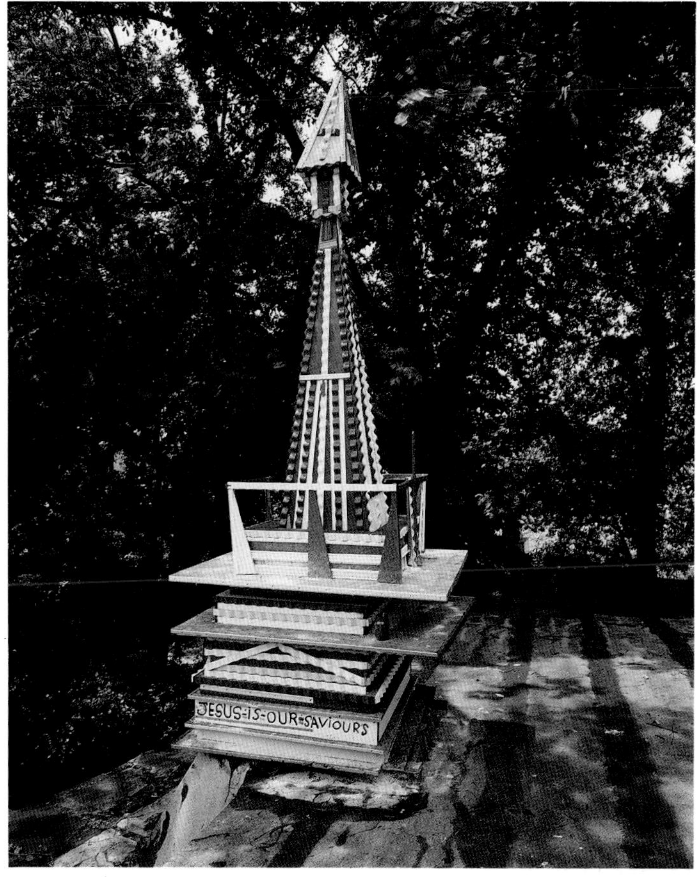

Obedian, to the great Head
of the Church
We're here by the profession
of your faith
Baptize you
In the name of the Father
Who is Jehovah
In the name of the Son

Steeple on Margaret's Market, Vicksburg, 1990

Which is Jesus Christ
In the name of the Holy
Ghost

With the words "in the name of the Holy Ghost," Reverend Meek, assisted by the two deacons, covered Obedian's nose and mouth and leaned him backward into the water. As Obedian rose from the watery grave, those gathered on the bank began to sing:

Didn't see nobody, but I felt
the change
I didn't see nobody, but I felt
the change

As the bell tower churches rot, as preachers pass on and congregations move out of the rural areas to towns and cities and as graves distinguished by handmade stones erode away, sink, and become overgrown, the Delta landscape will assume a different look. In the end, though, the real change will be signaled not by what is absent but by what is present—what takes the place of those old churches and pastors and hallowed grounds, what monuments are put there by new generations and new congregations whose hearts and hands were guided to create them just so.

Sacred Space

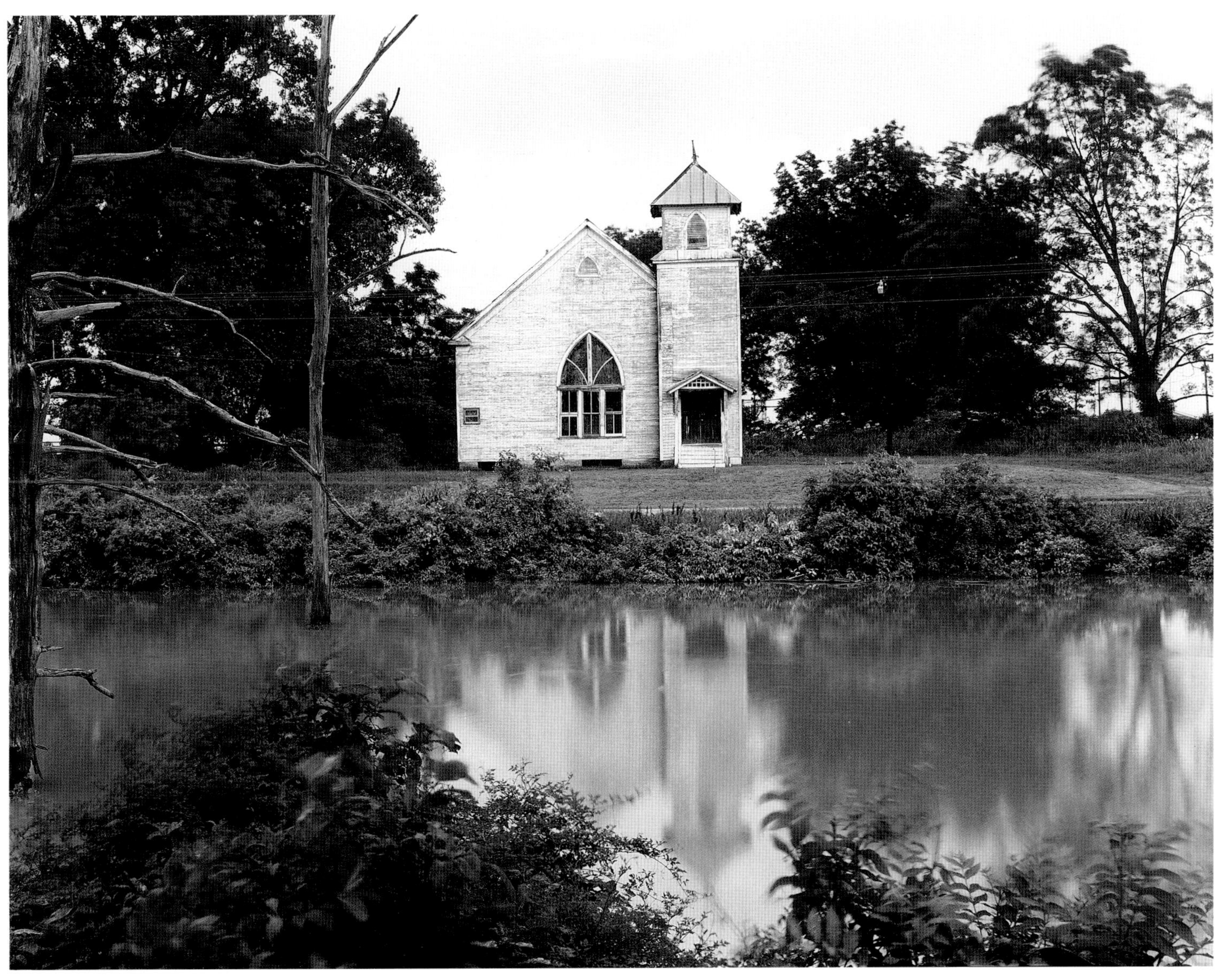

Estill, 1989

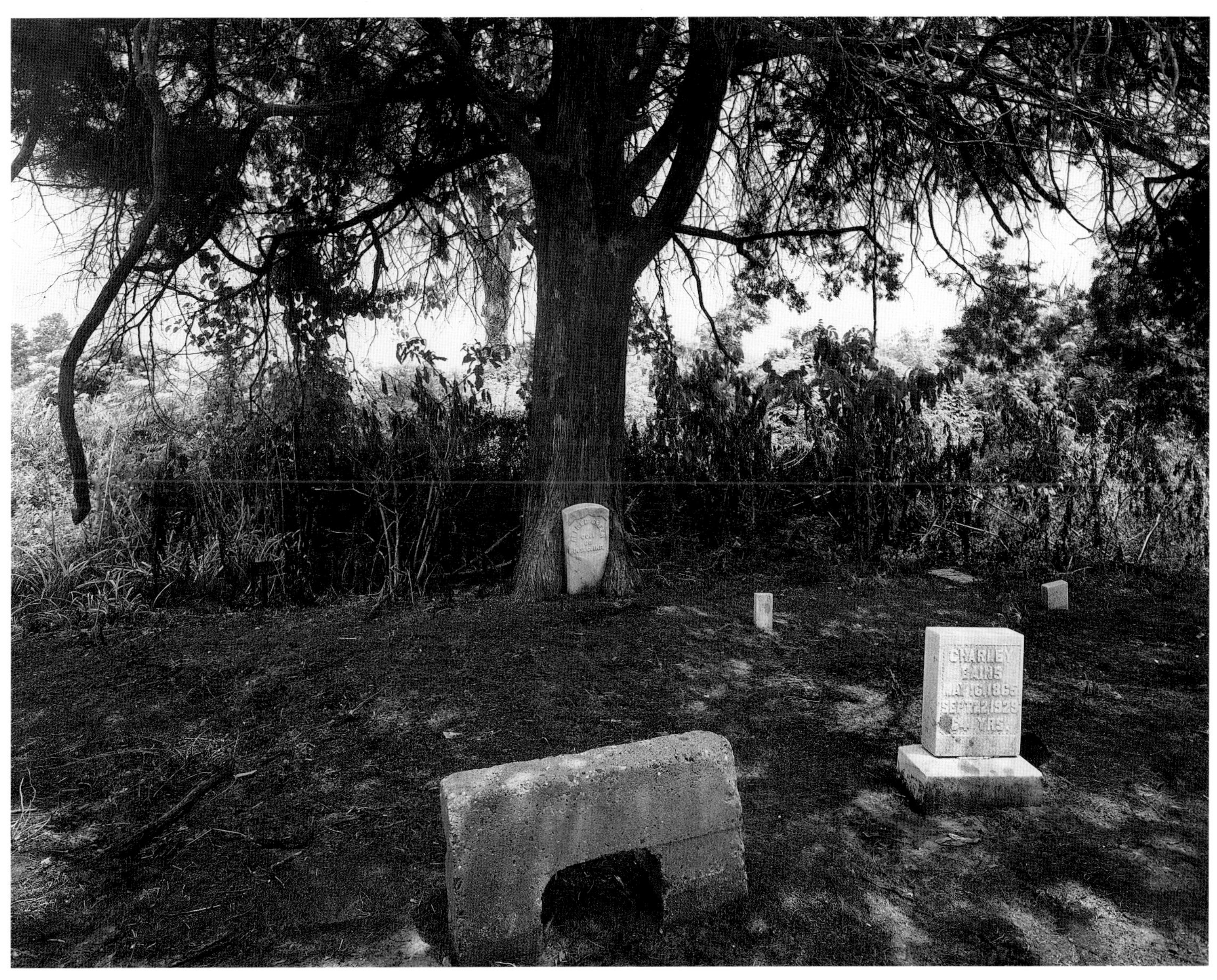

Cemetery, Morning Star M. B. Church, Beulah, 1989

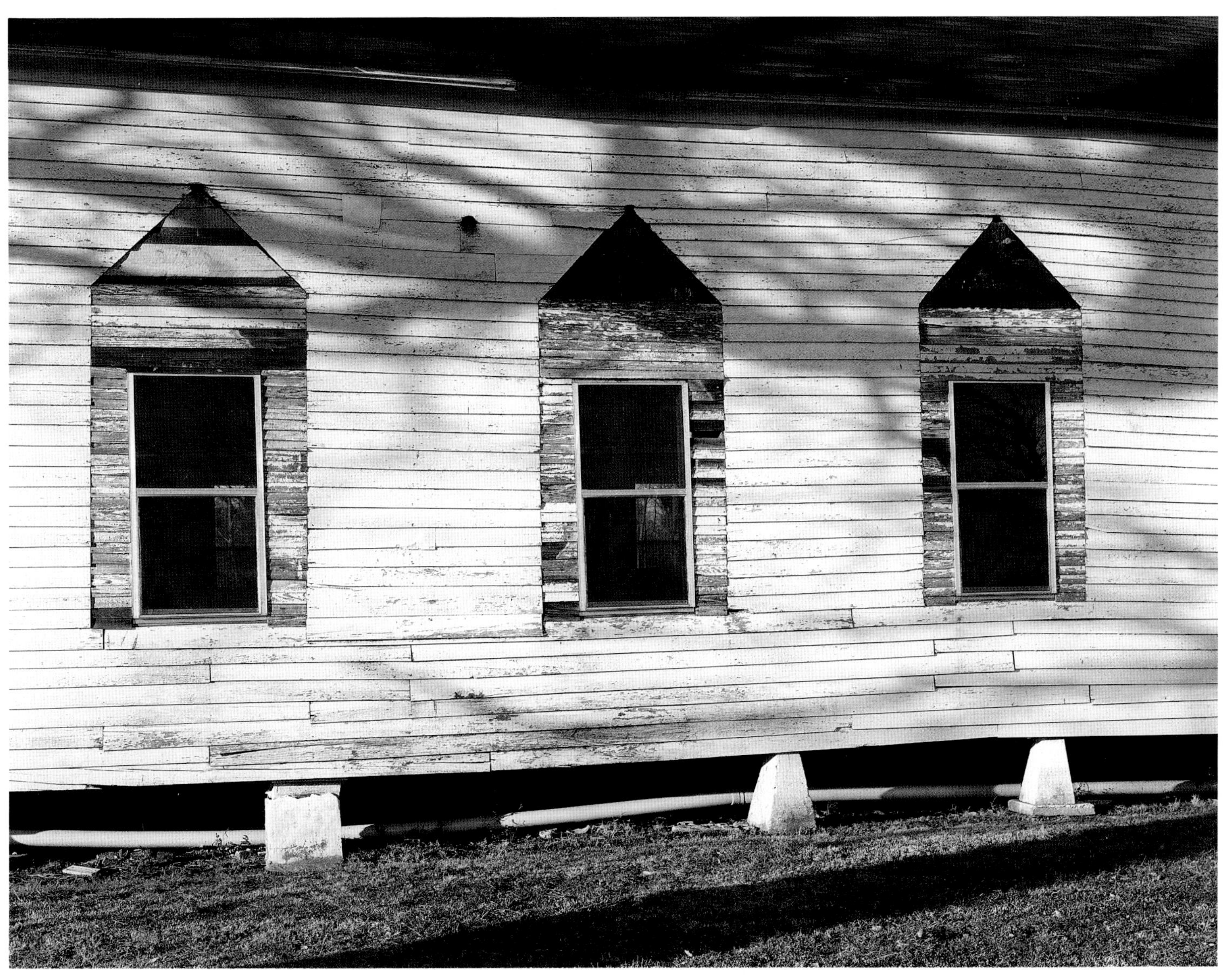

True Light M. B. Church,
Dockery, 1990

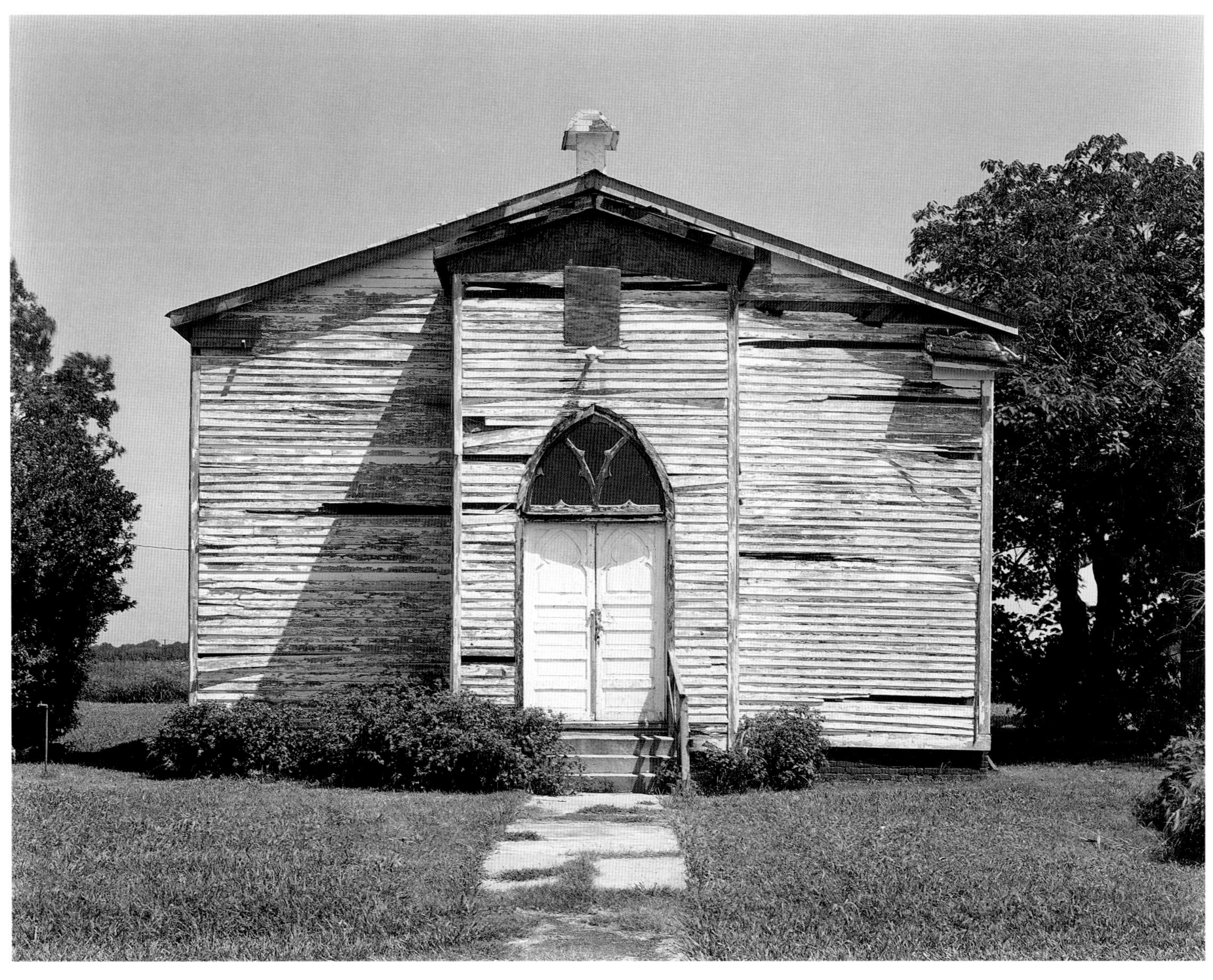

Mt. Airy M. B. Church, Friars
Point, 1990

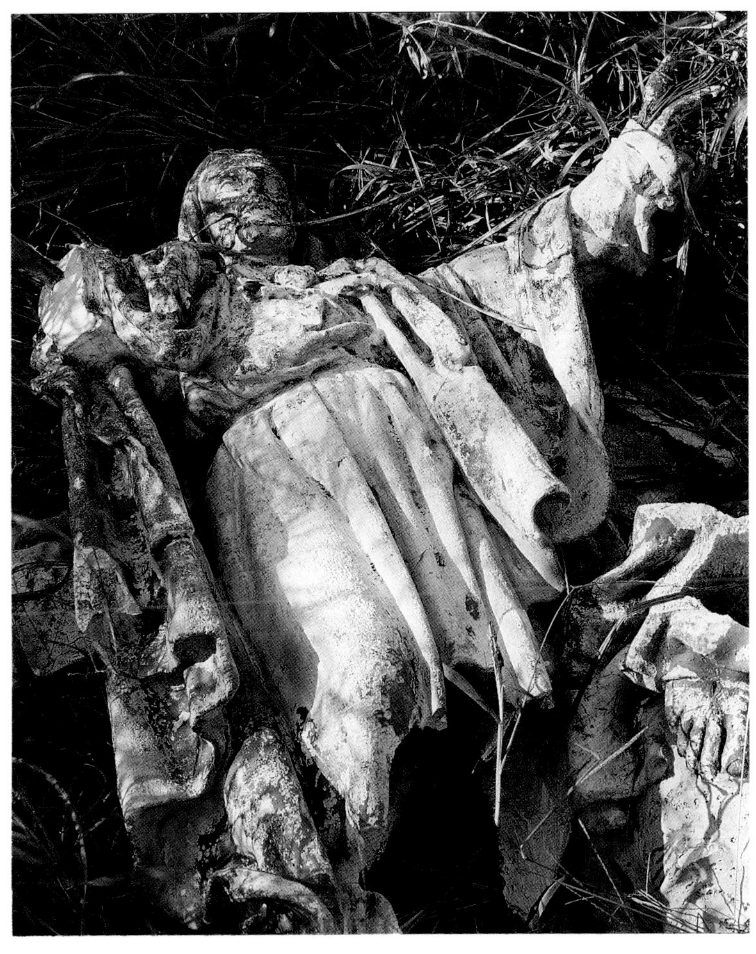

Cemetery, Mt. Airy, Friars Point, 1989

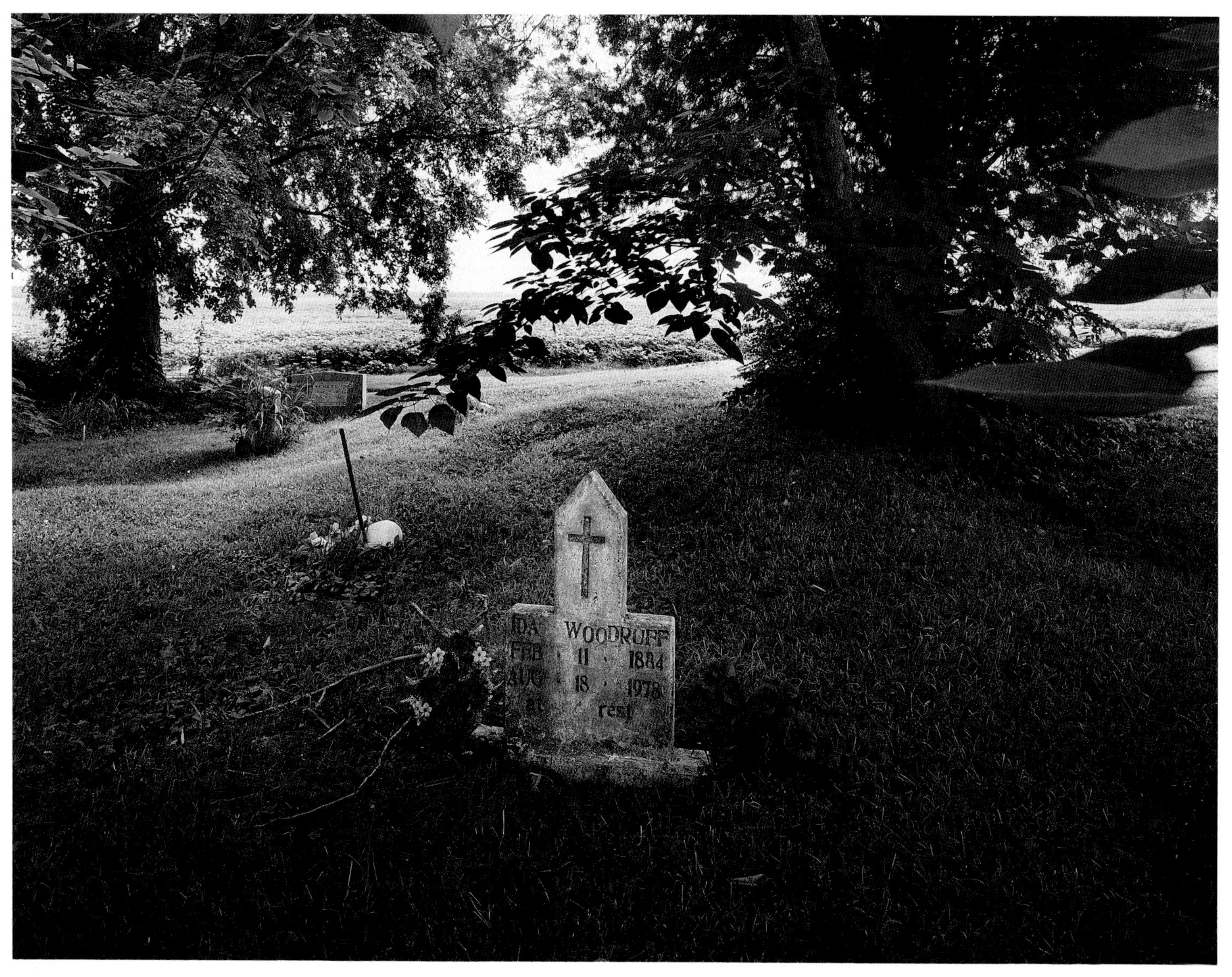

Near Shelby, 1989

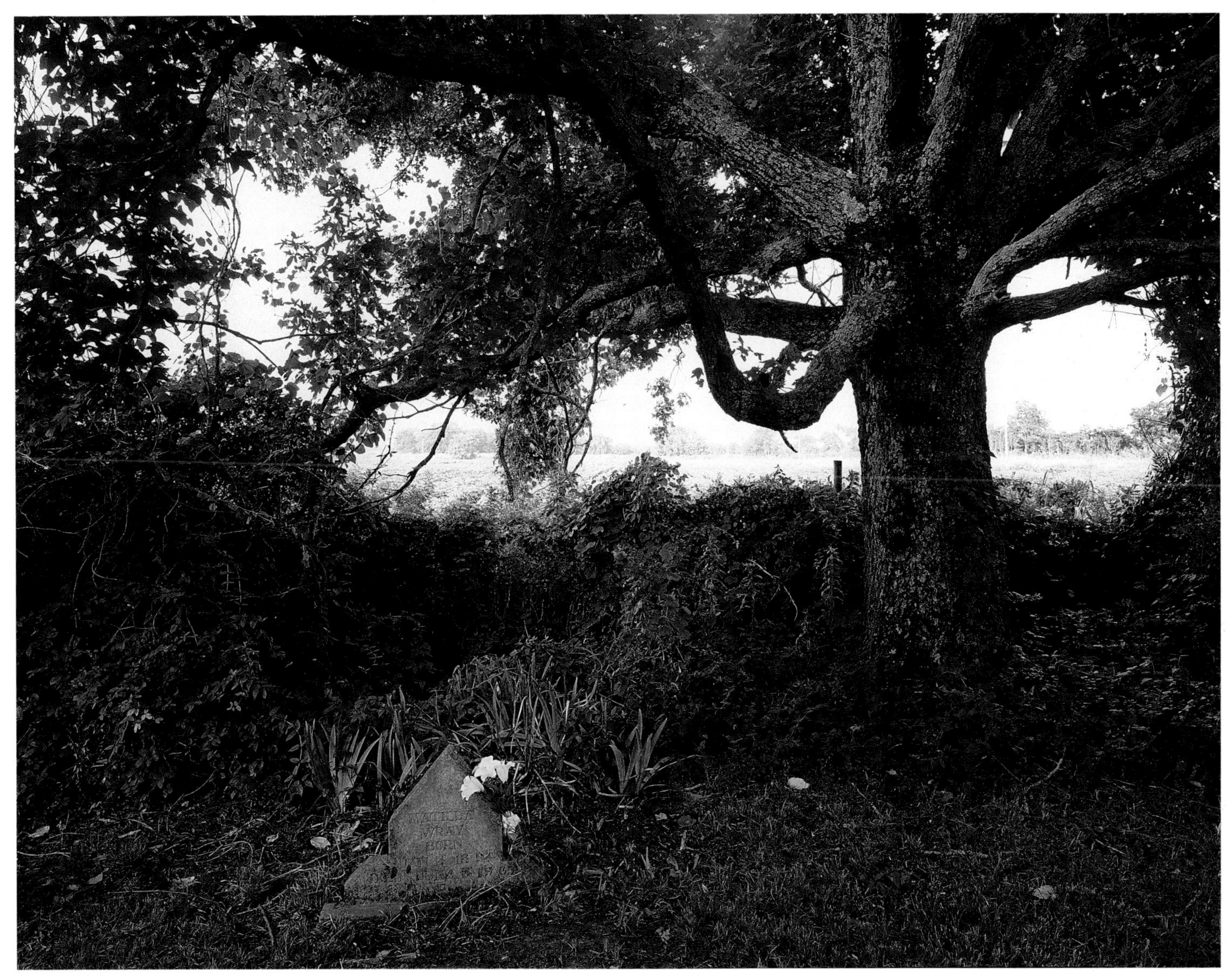

Near Shaw, 1990

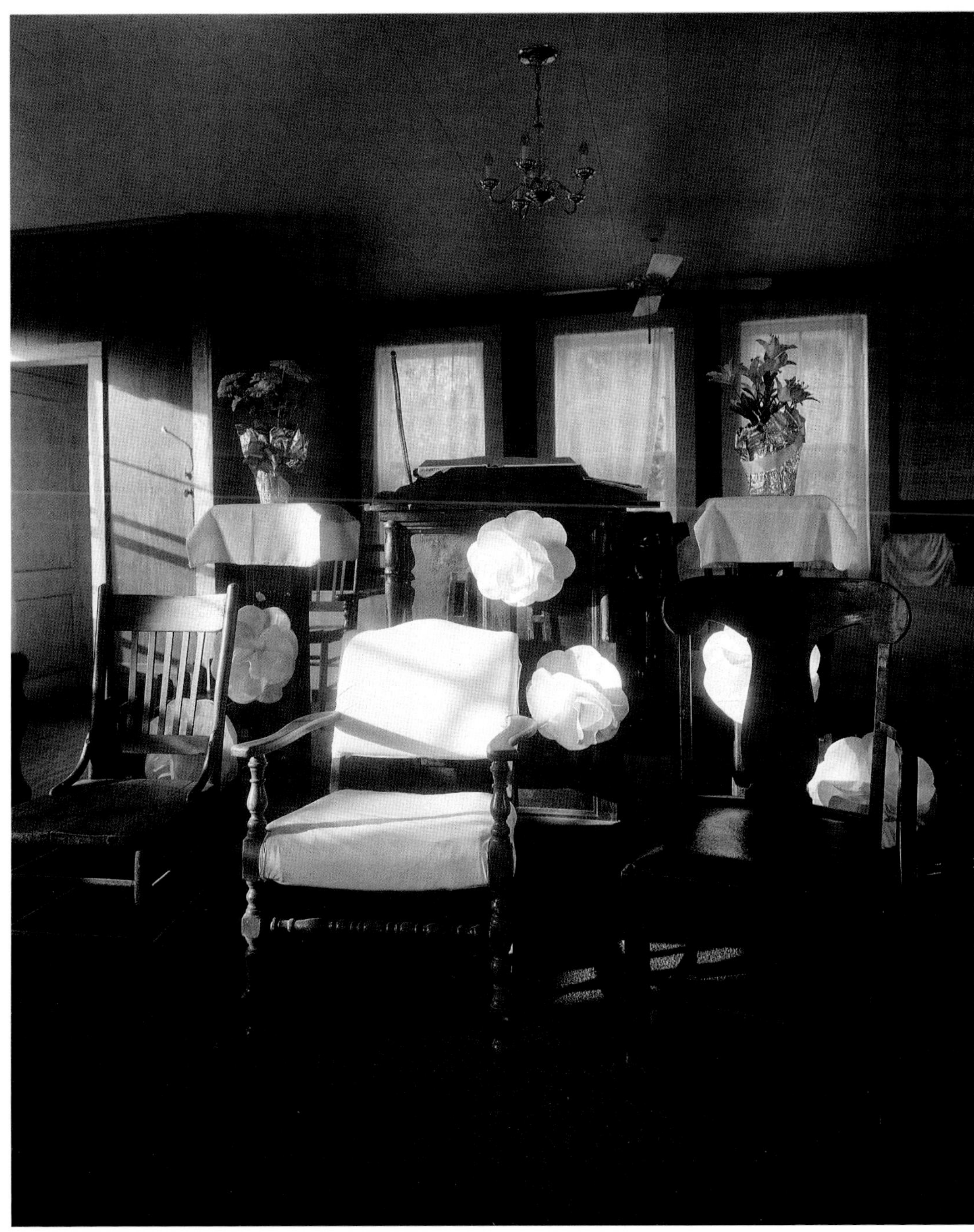

Paper Easter flowers, near Tchula, 1991

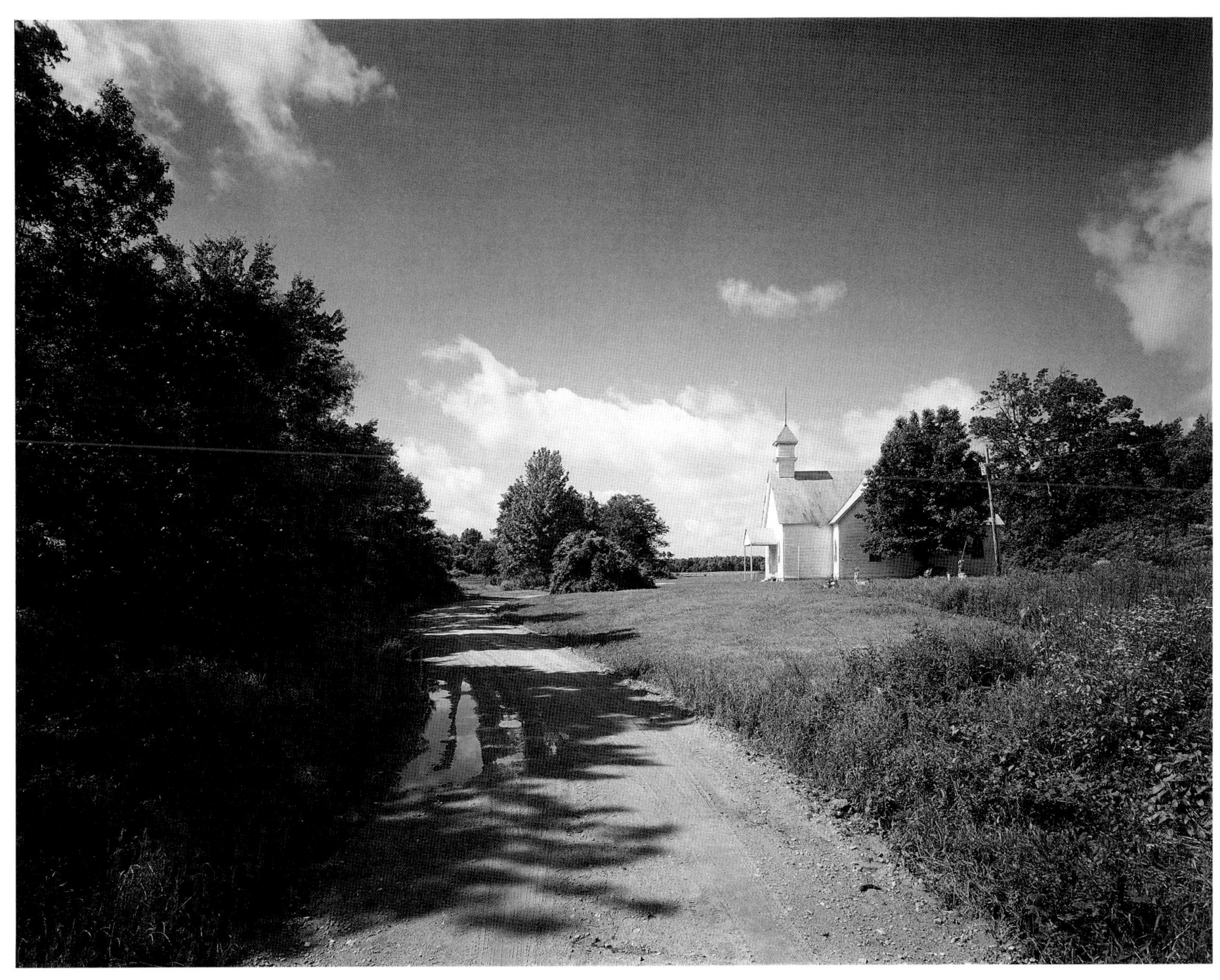

St. James M. B. Church,
Jonestown, 1991

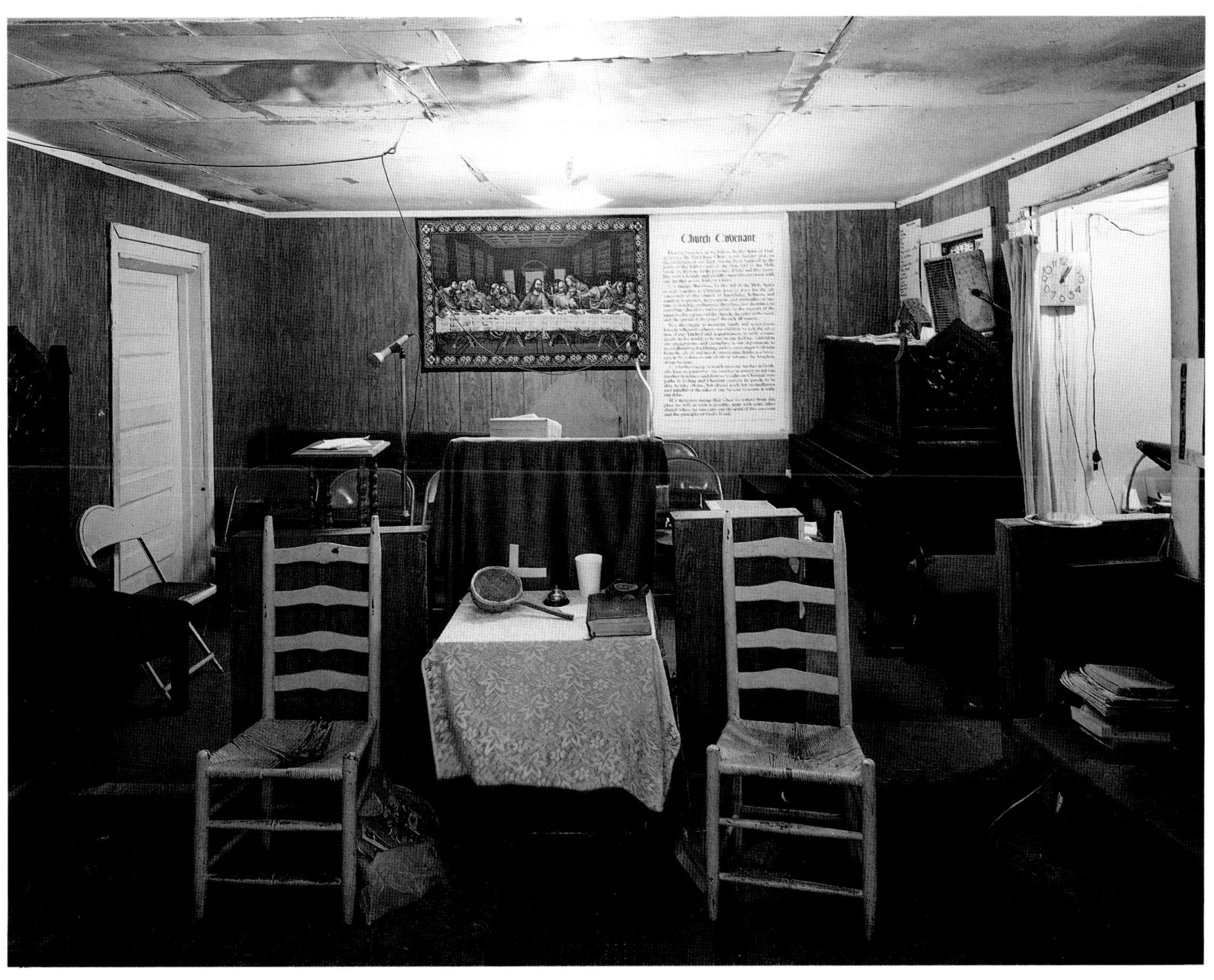

Little Ebenezer Baptist Church,
Rosedale, 1990

Bethlehem No. 2 M. B. Church,
Shaw, 1992

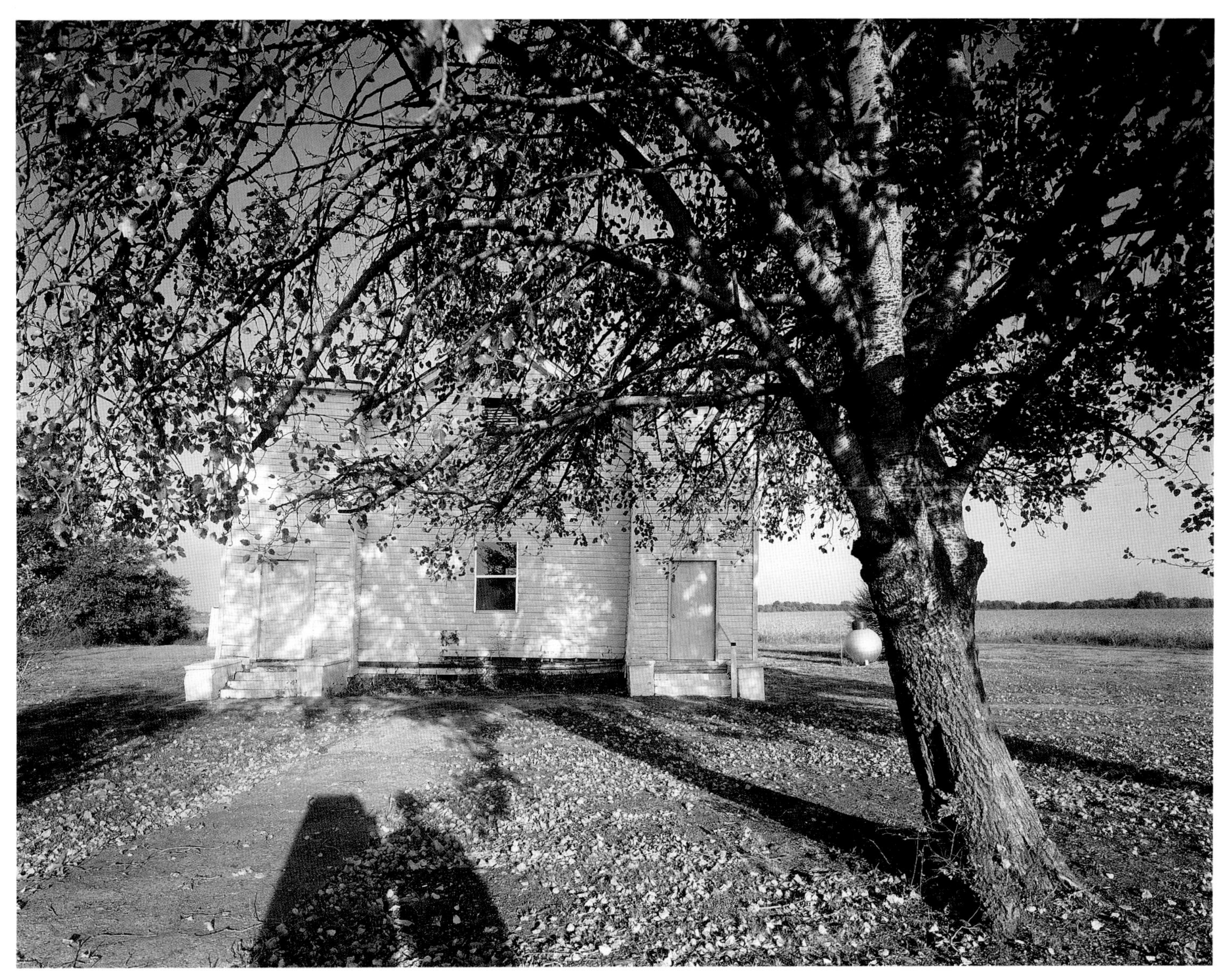

DeLoach Road, Alligator, 1992

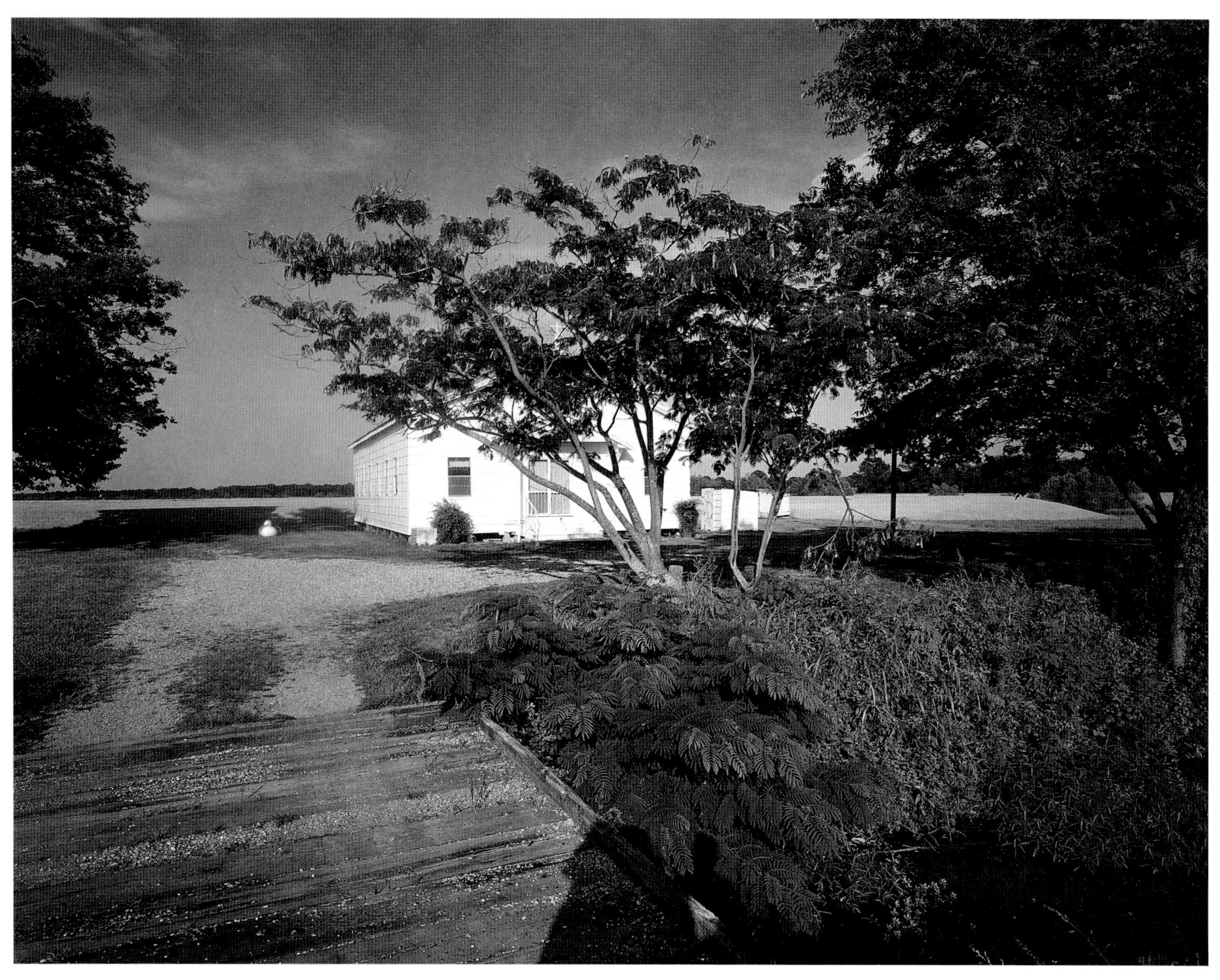

Sunflower County, 1991

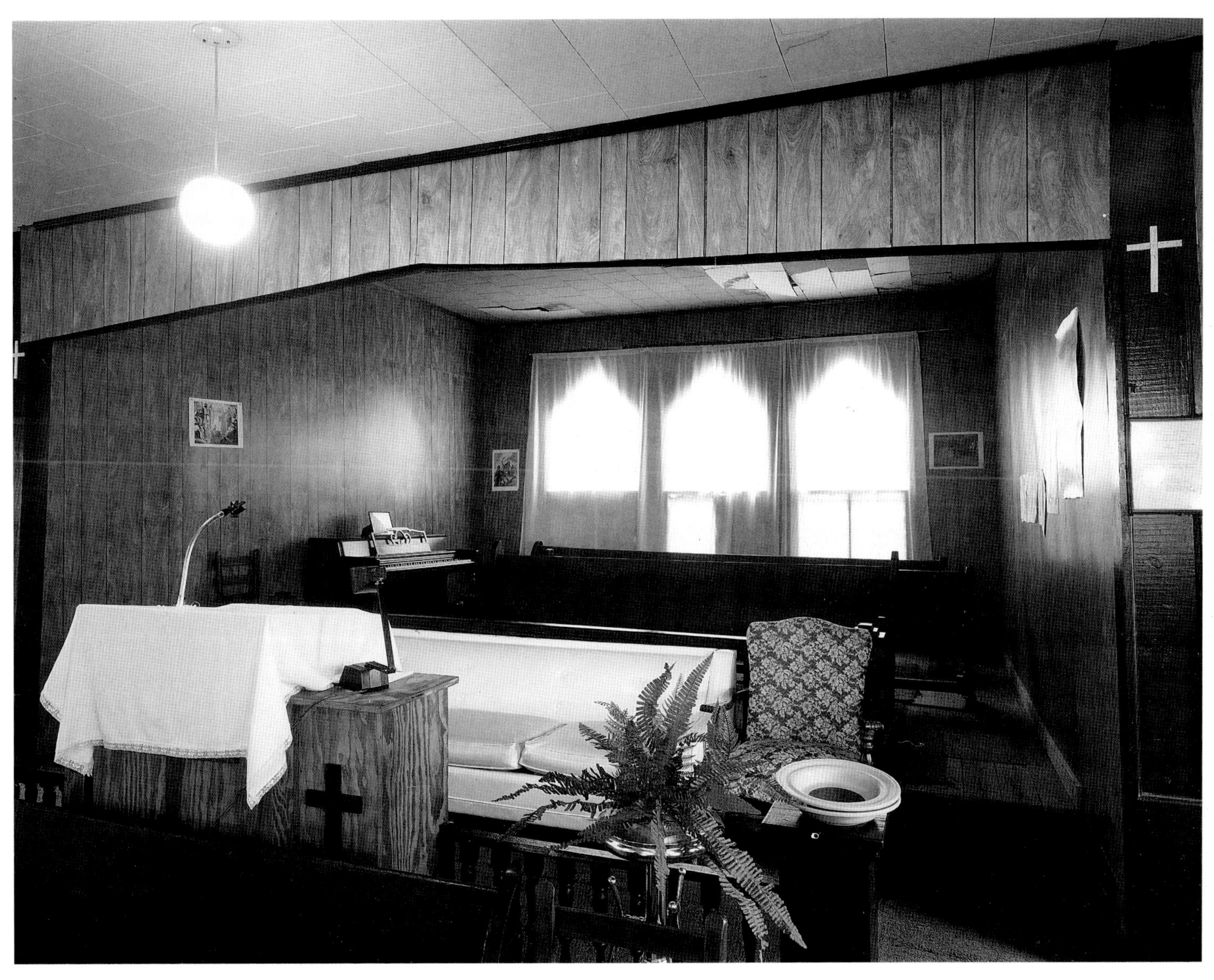

True Light M. B. Church,
Dockery, 1989

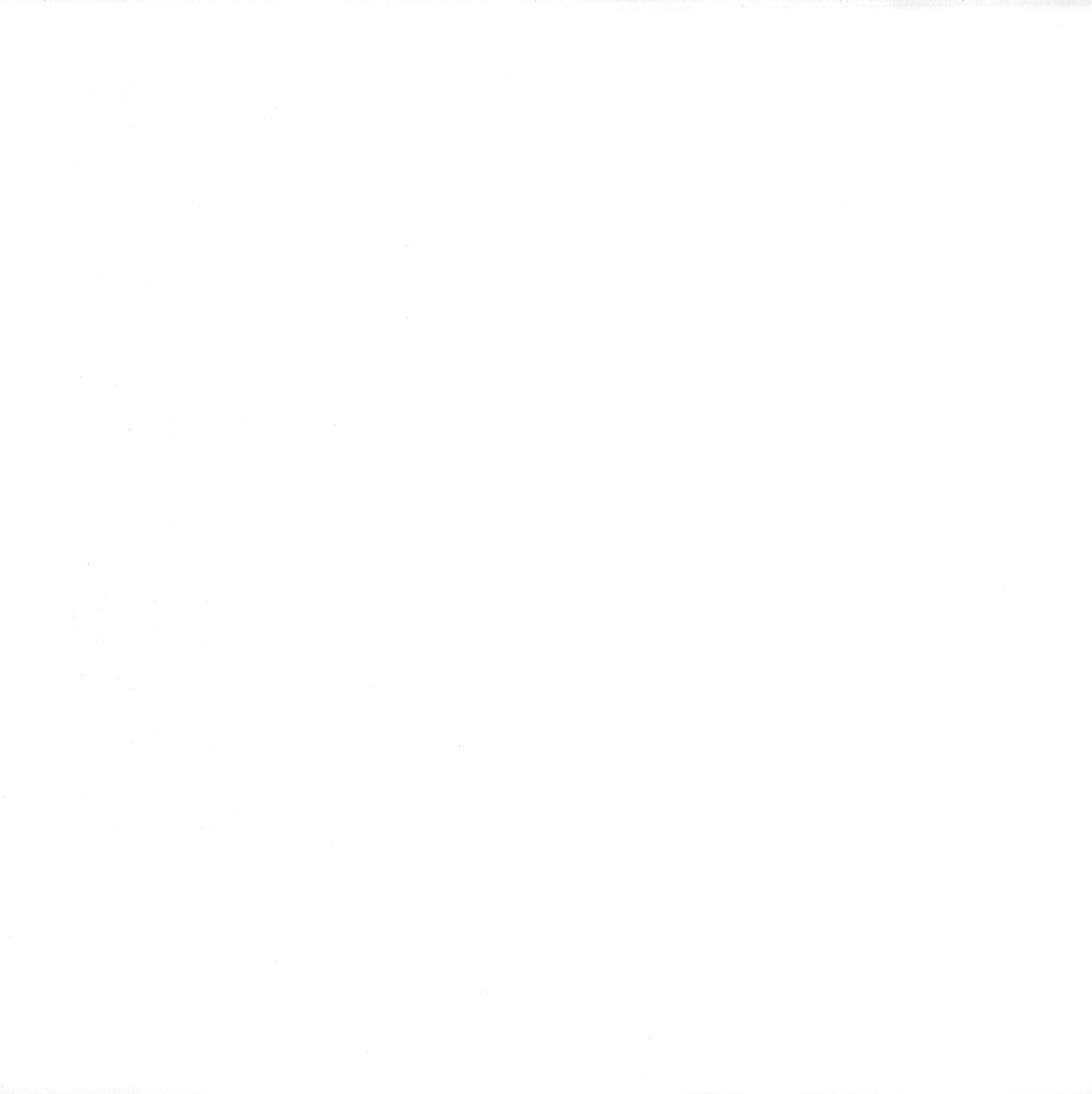

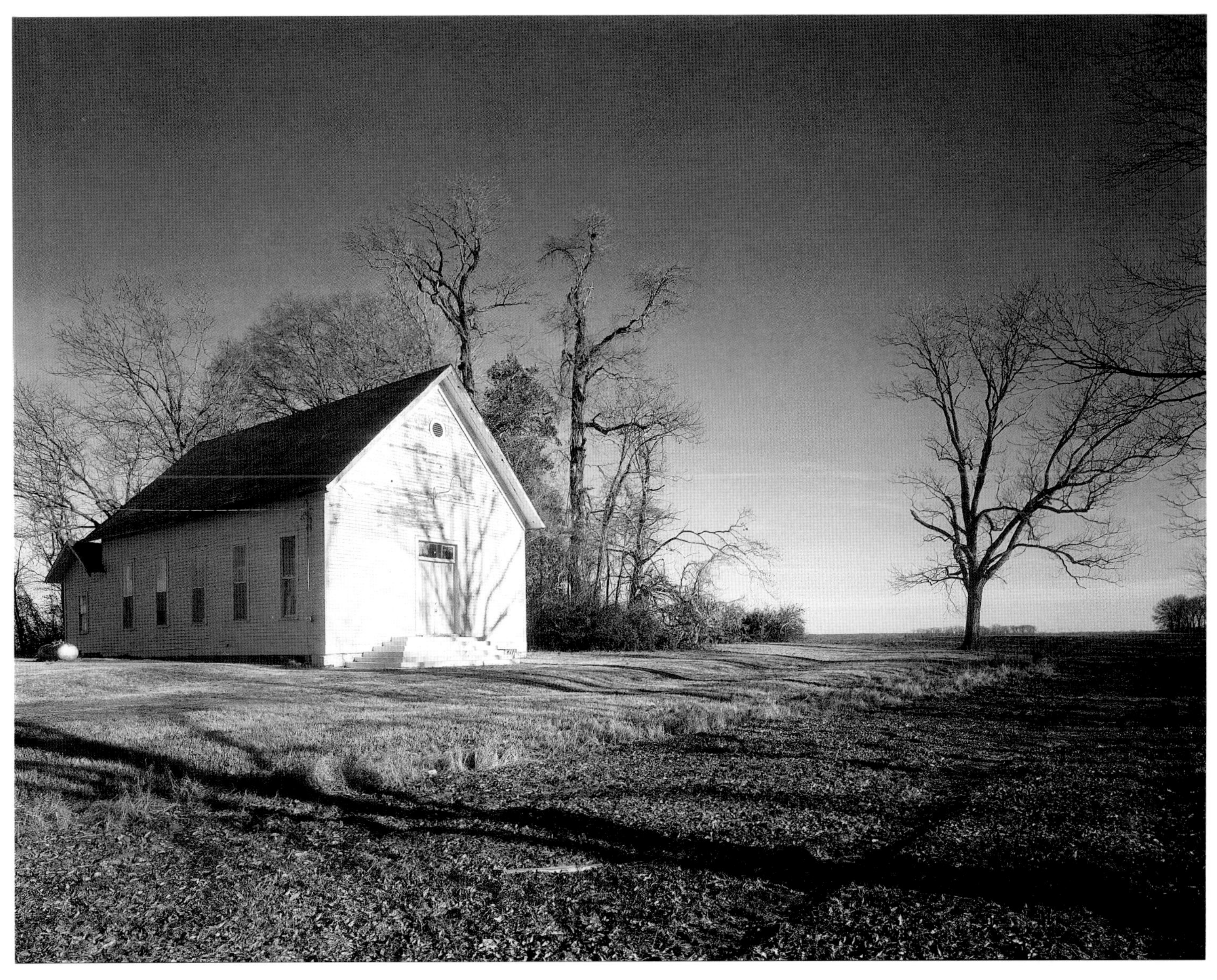

Shellmound, 1991

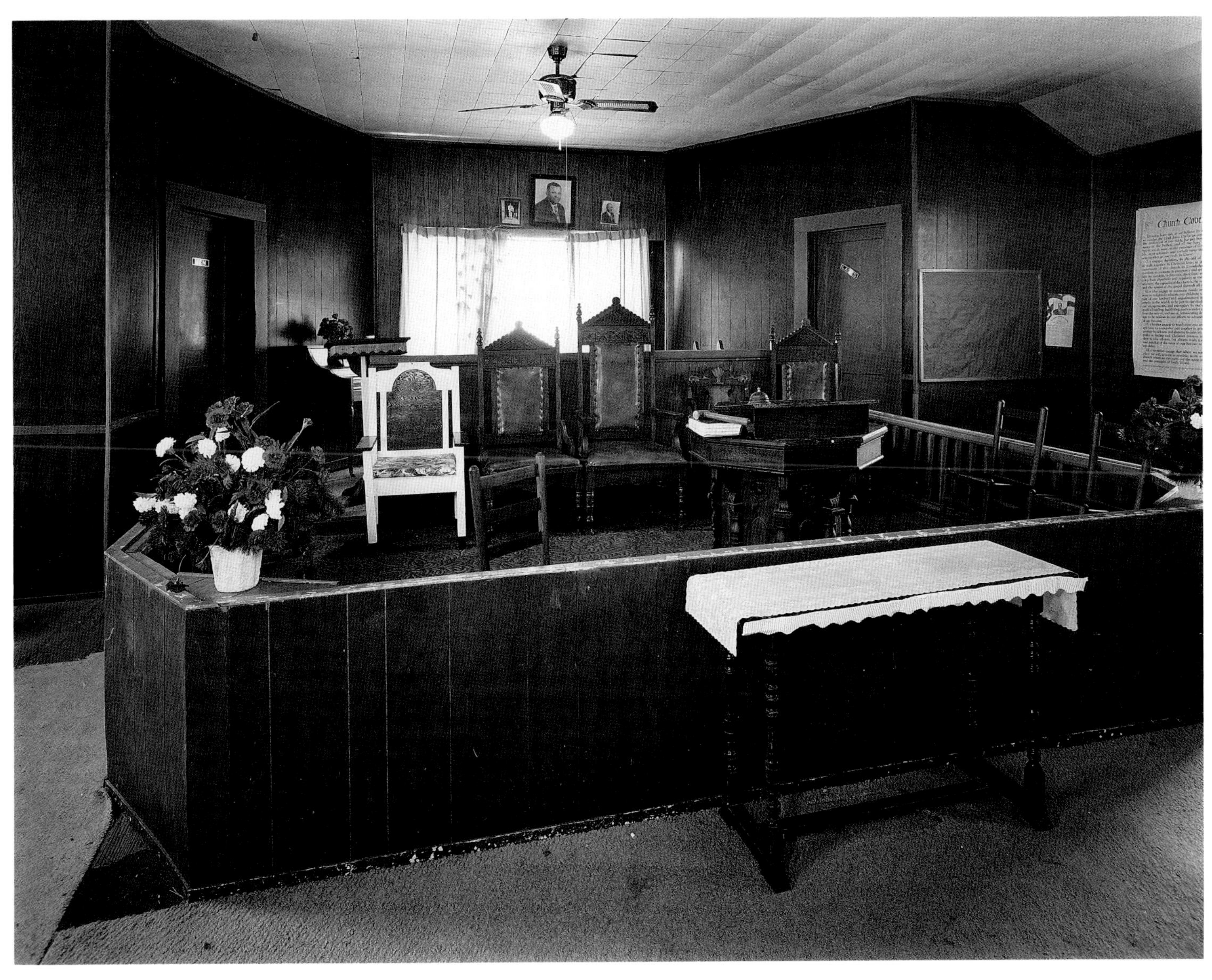

Pleasant Green M. B. Church,
Rolling Fork, 1989

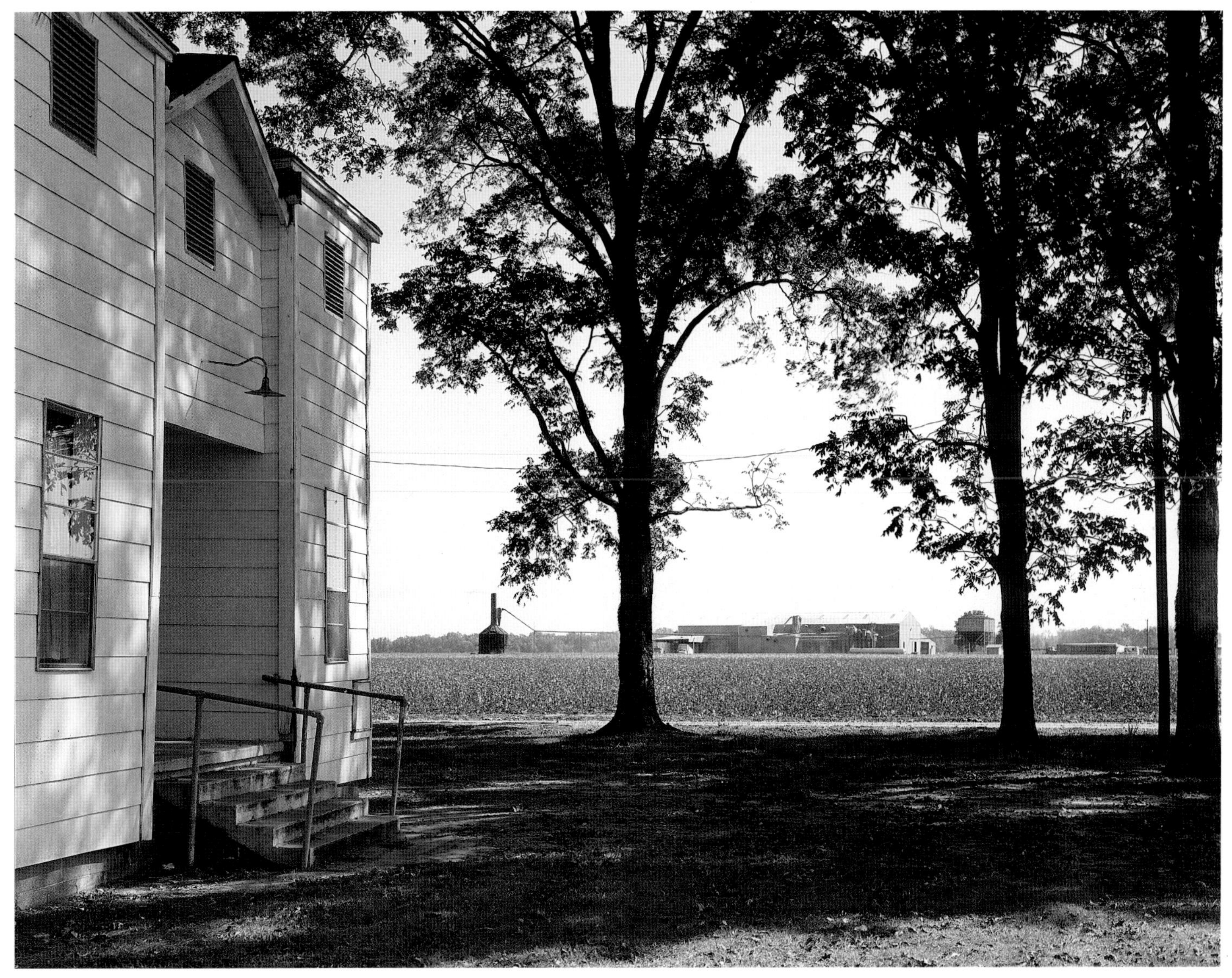

Holly Bluff, 1990

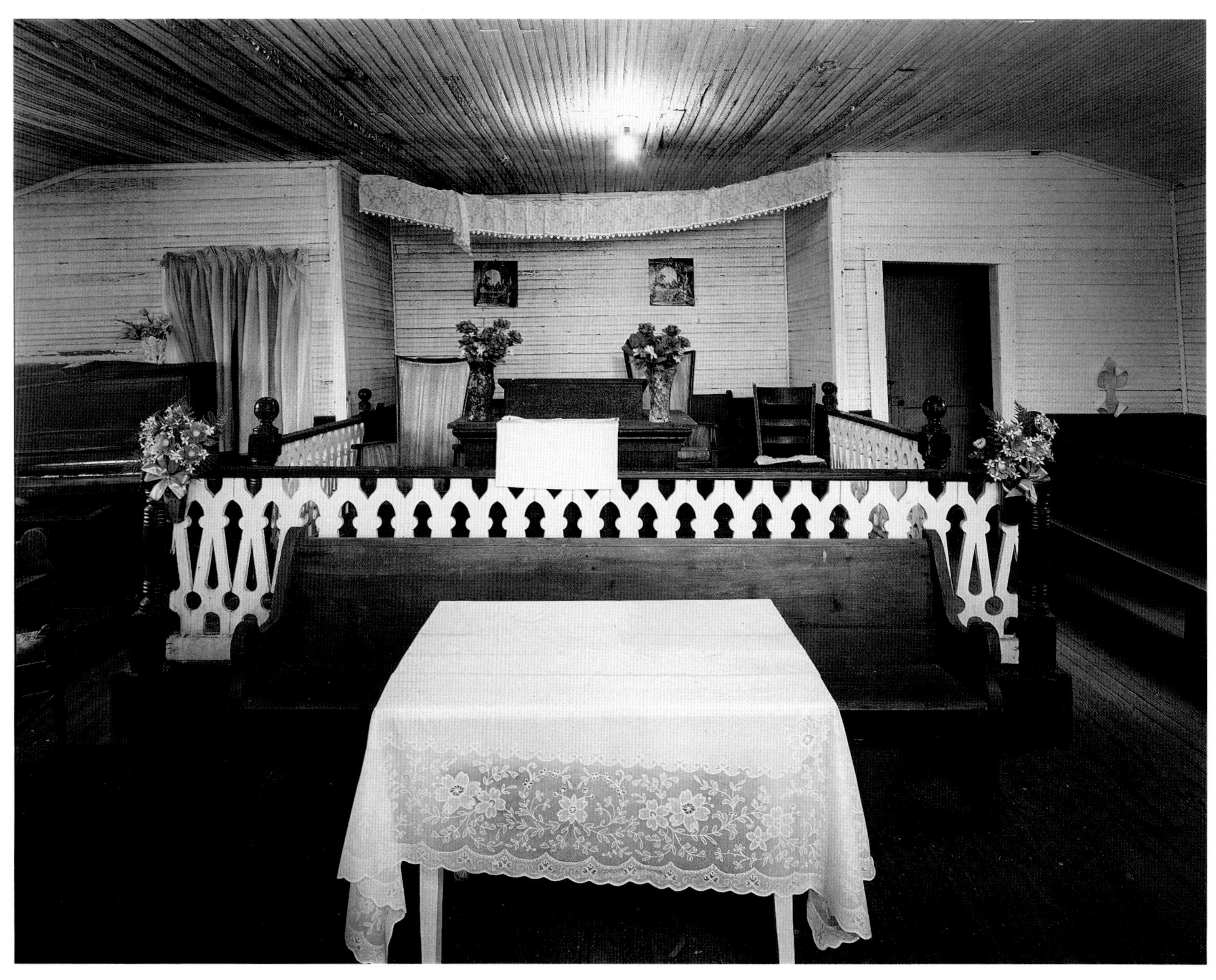

New Hope Church, Shelby, 1989

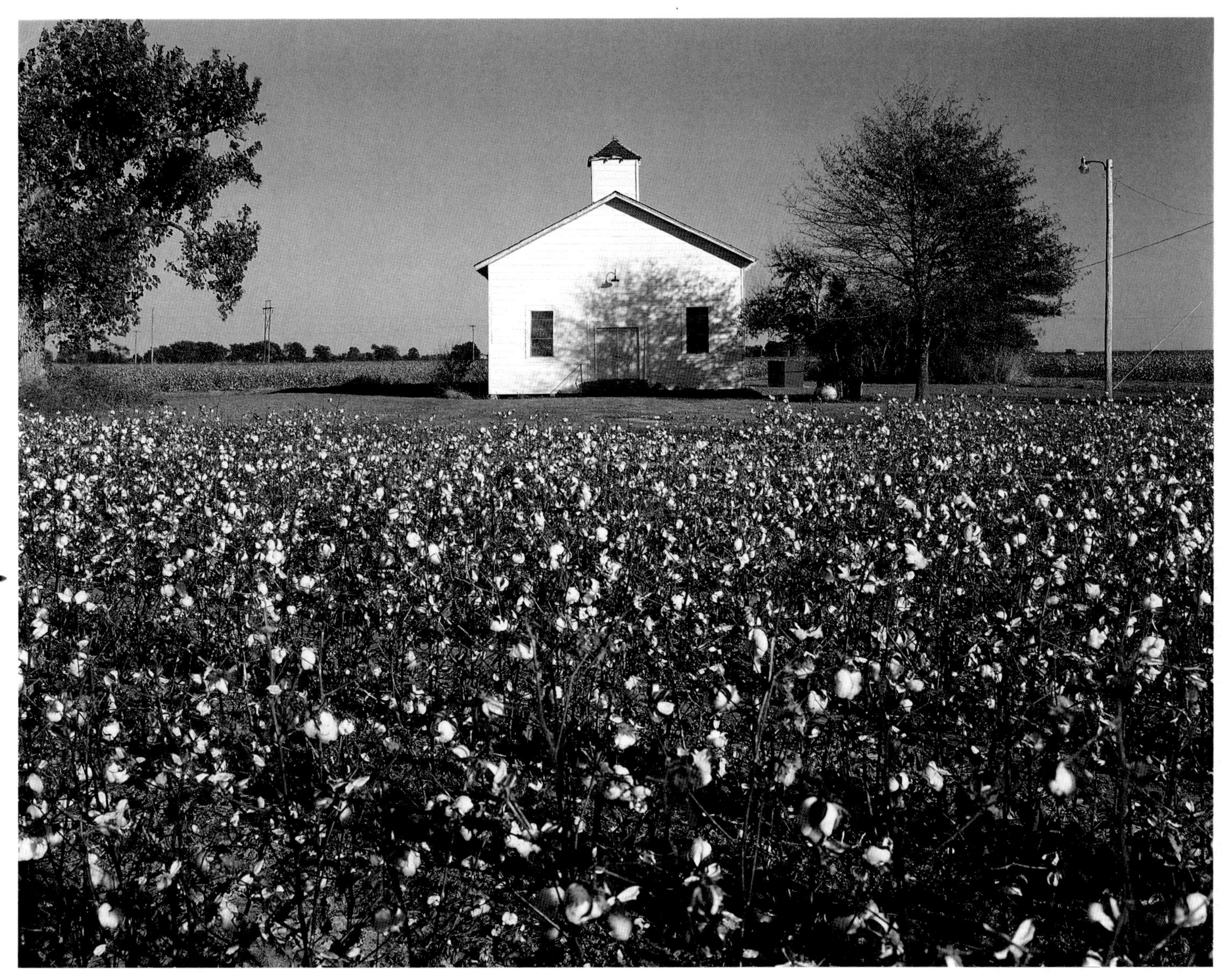

Pleasant Green M. B. Church,
Rolling Fork, 1990

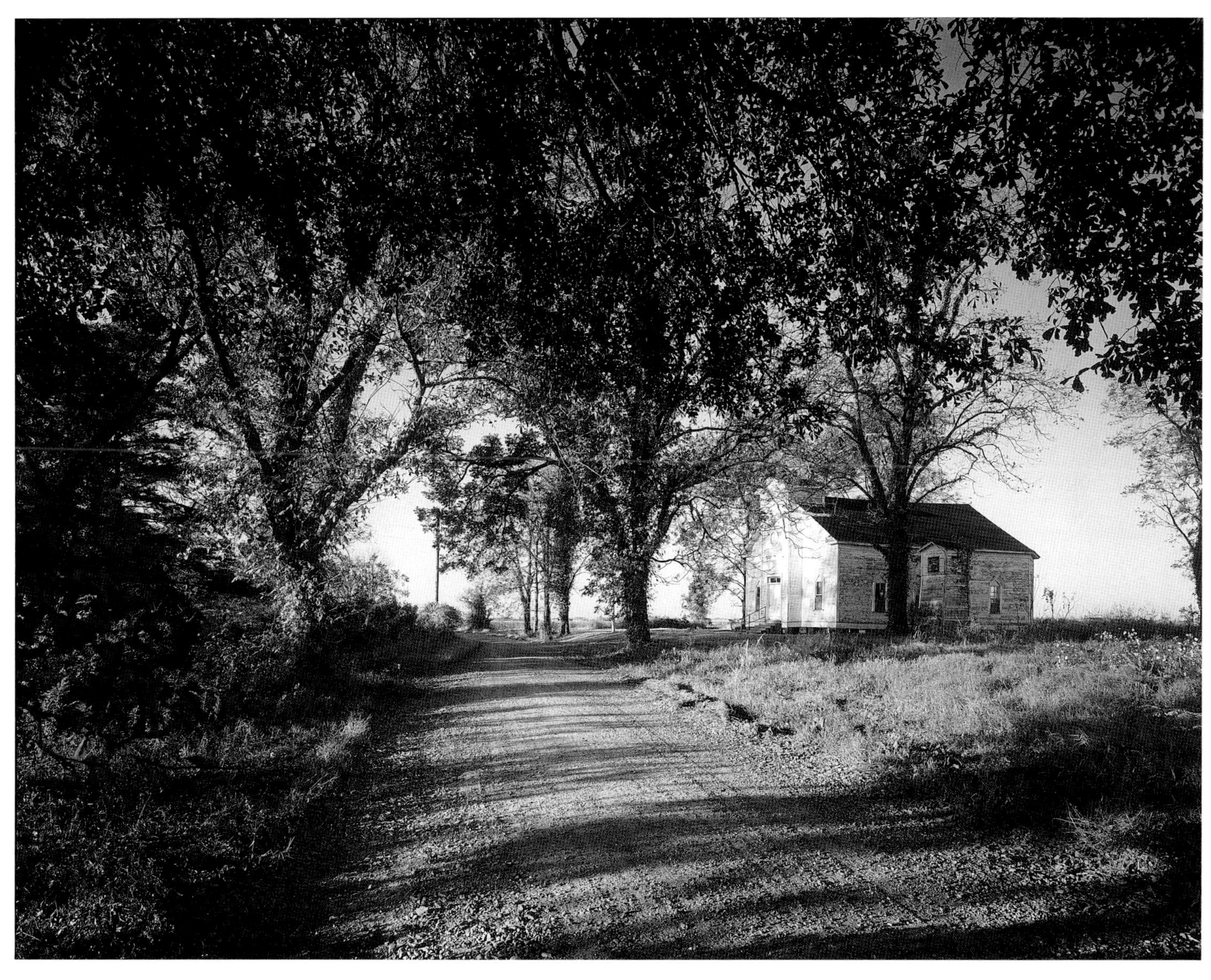

Bethlehem No. 2 M. B. Church,
Shaw, 1991

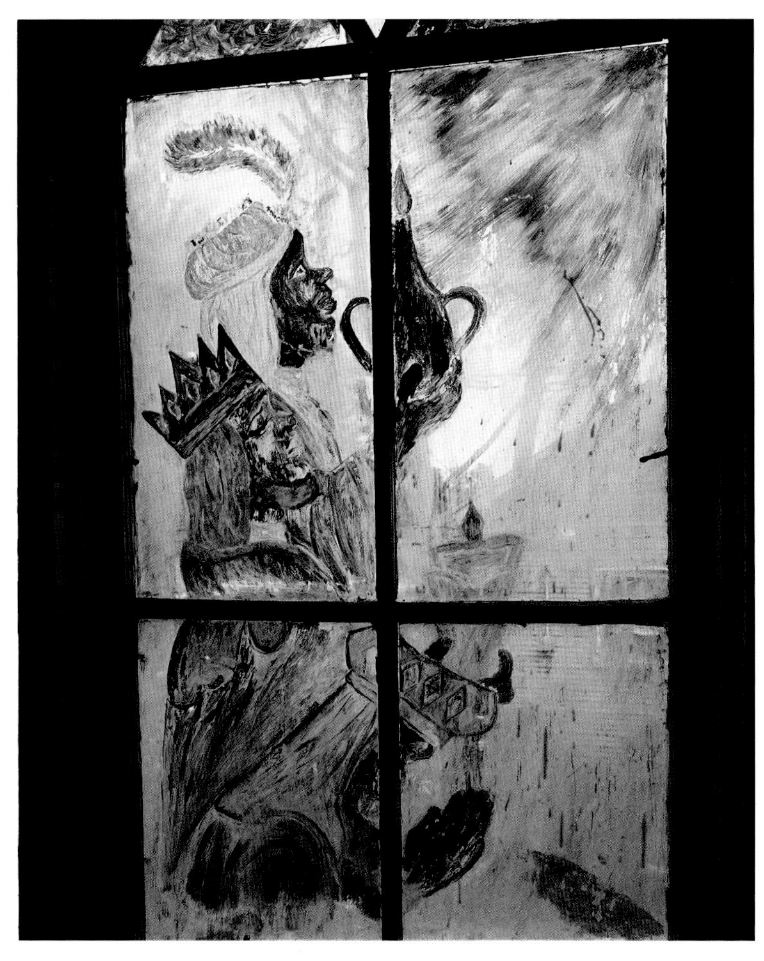

Hand-painted window, A.M.E. Church, Indianola, 1990

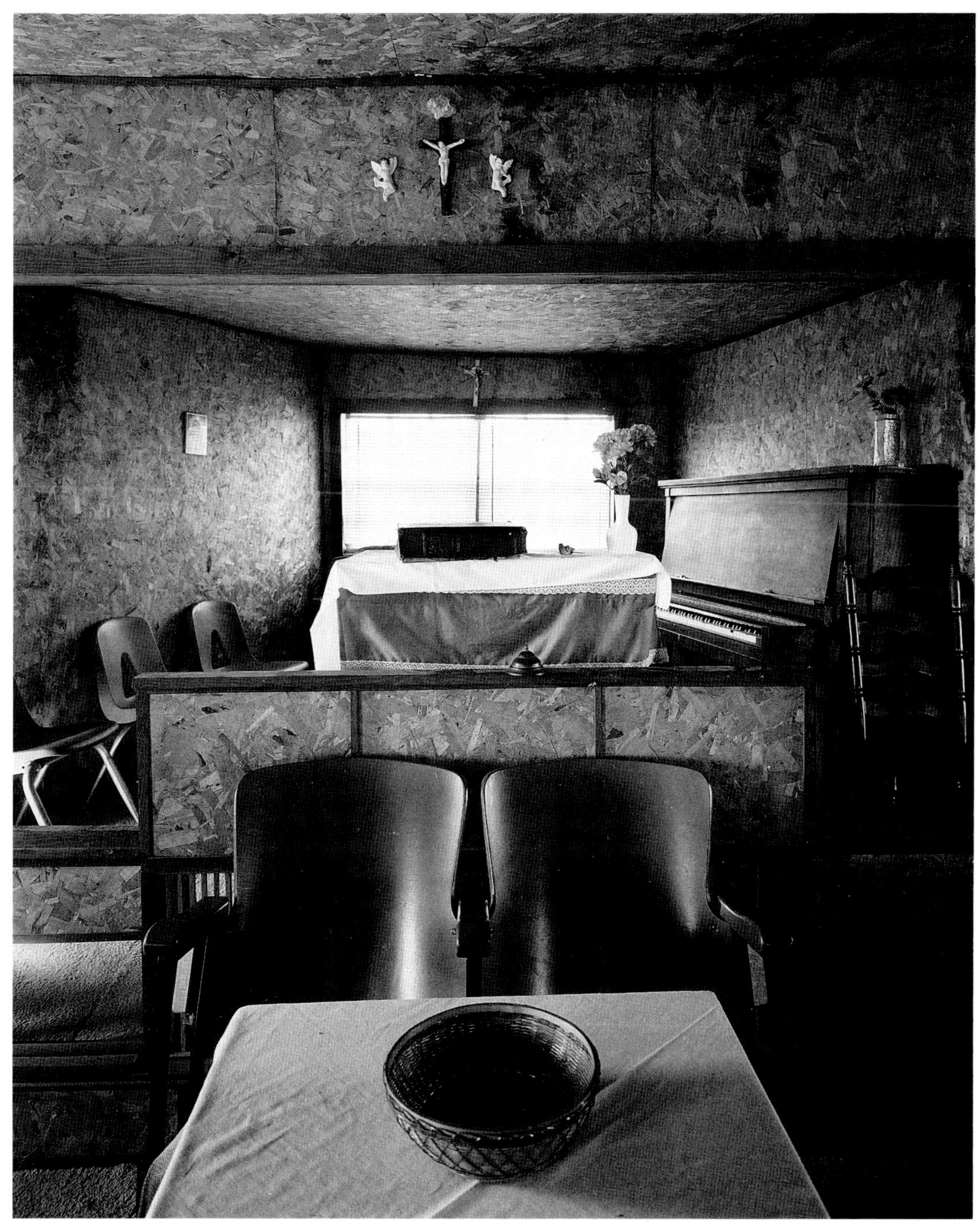

Mt. Olive church, near Beulah, 1992

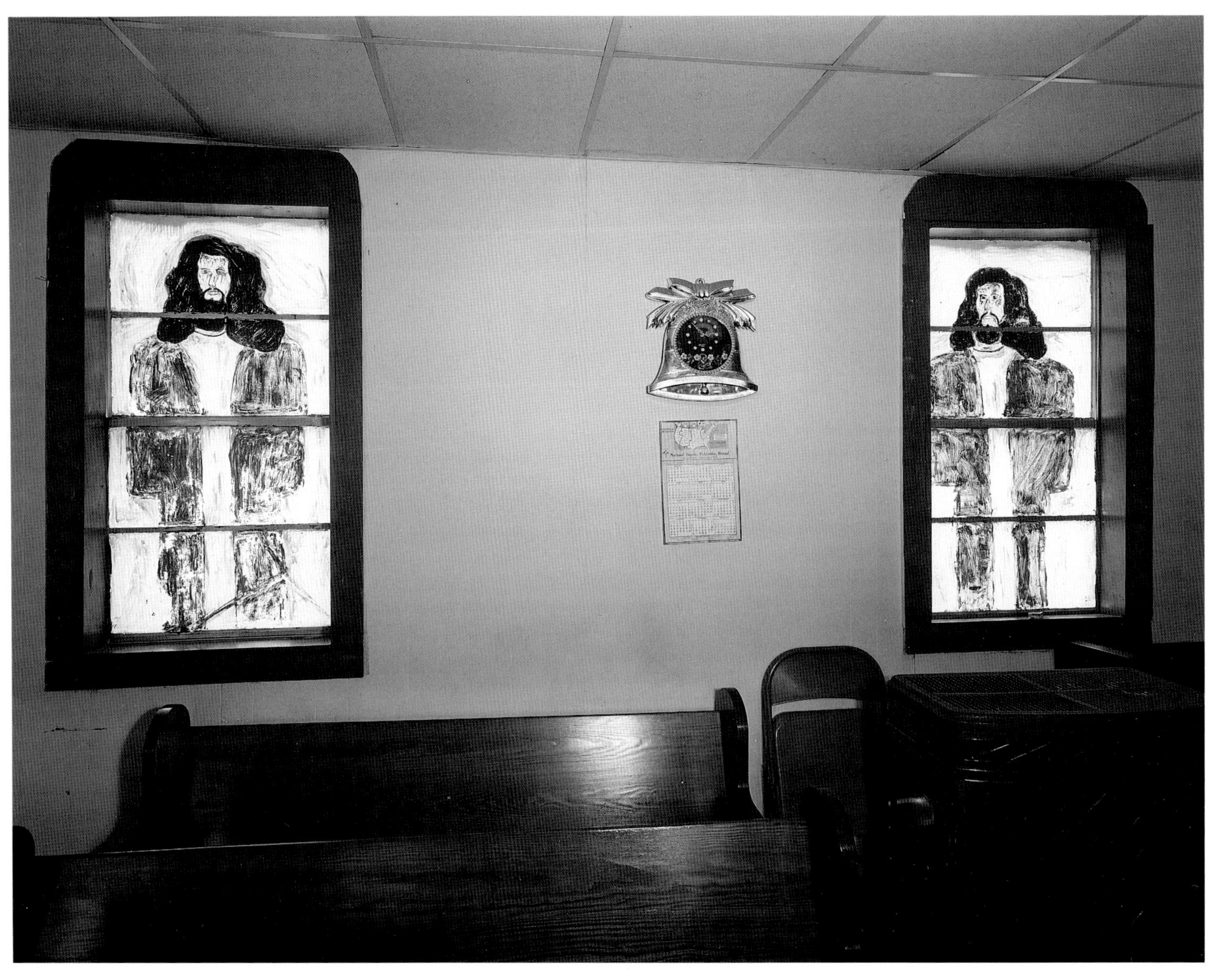

Chester Arthur Burke Memorial
M. B. Church, Rosedale, 1989

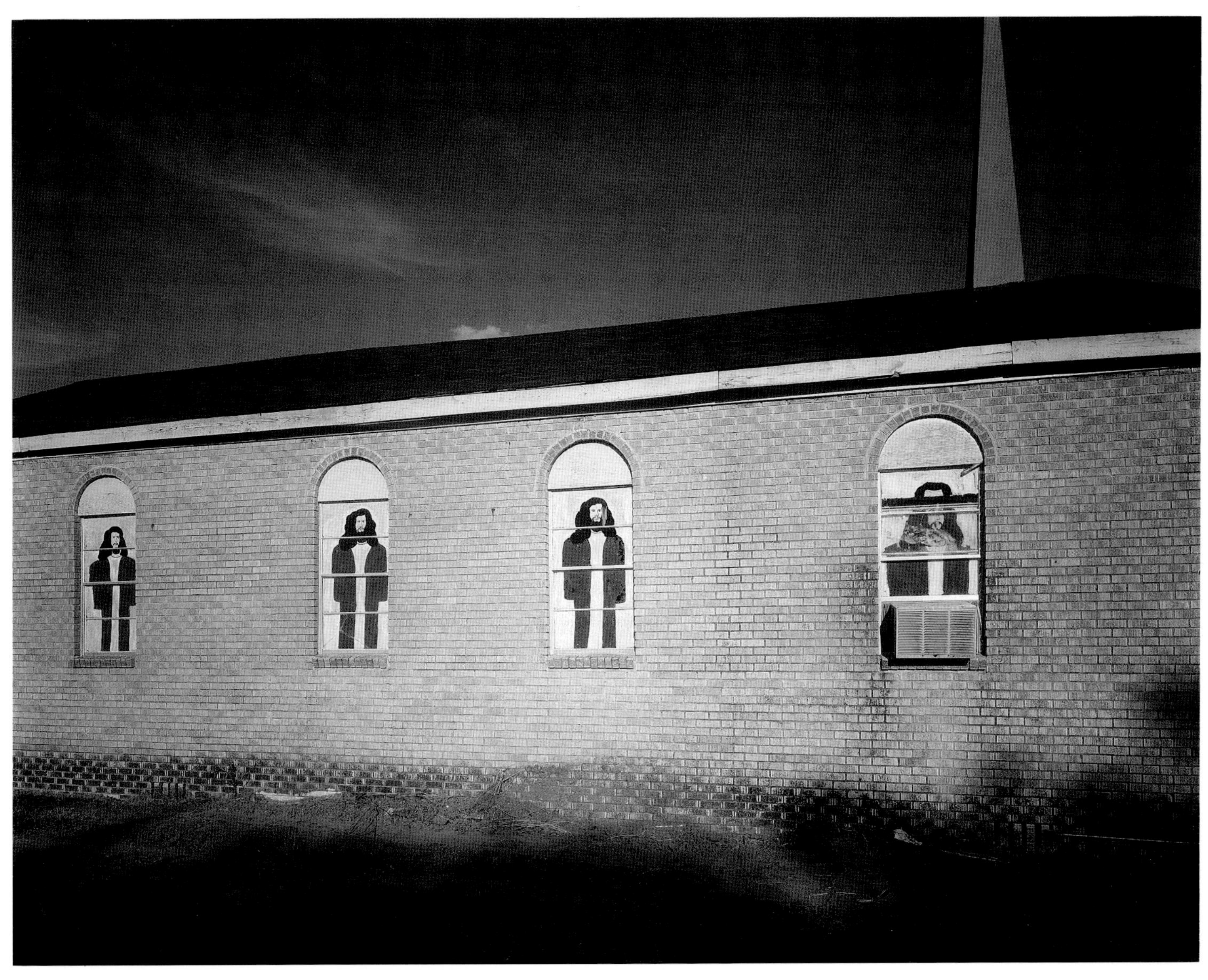

C. A. Burke Memorial M. B.
Church, Rosedale, 1989

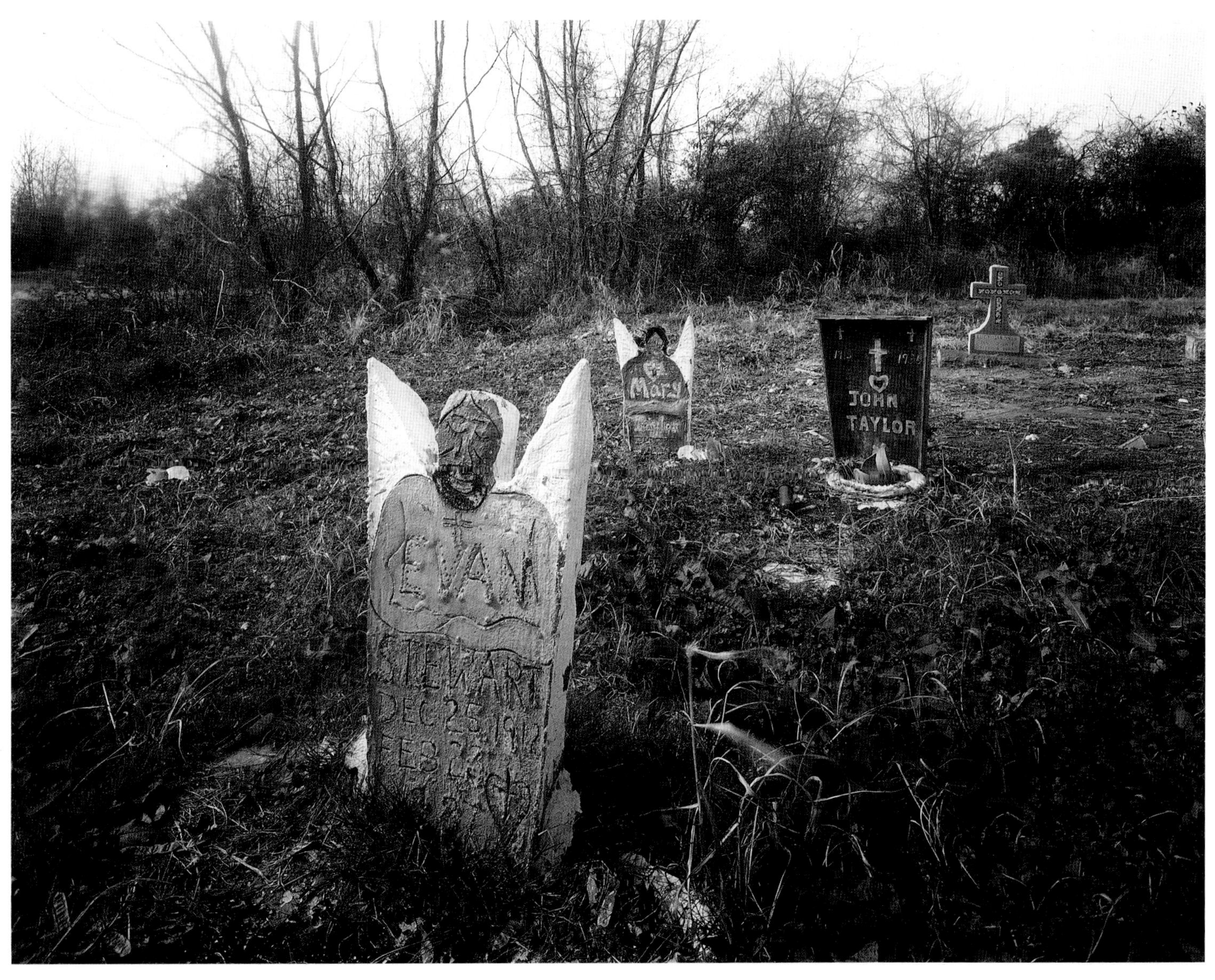

Handmade gravestones, Mound Bayou, 1989

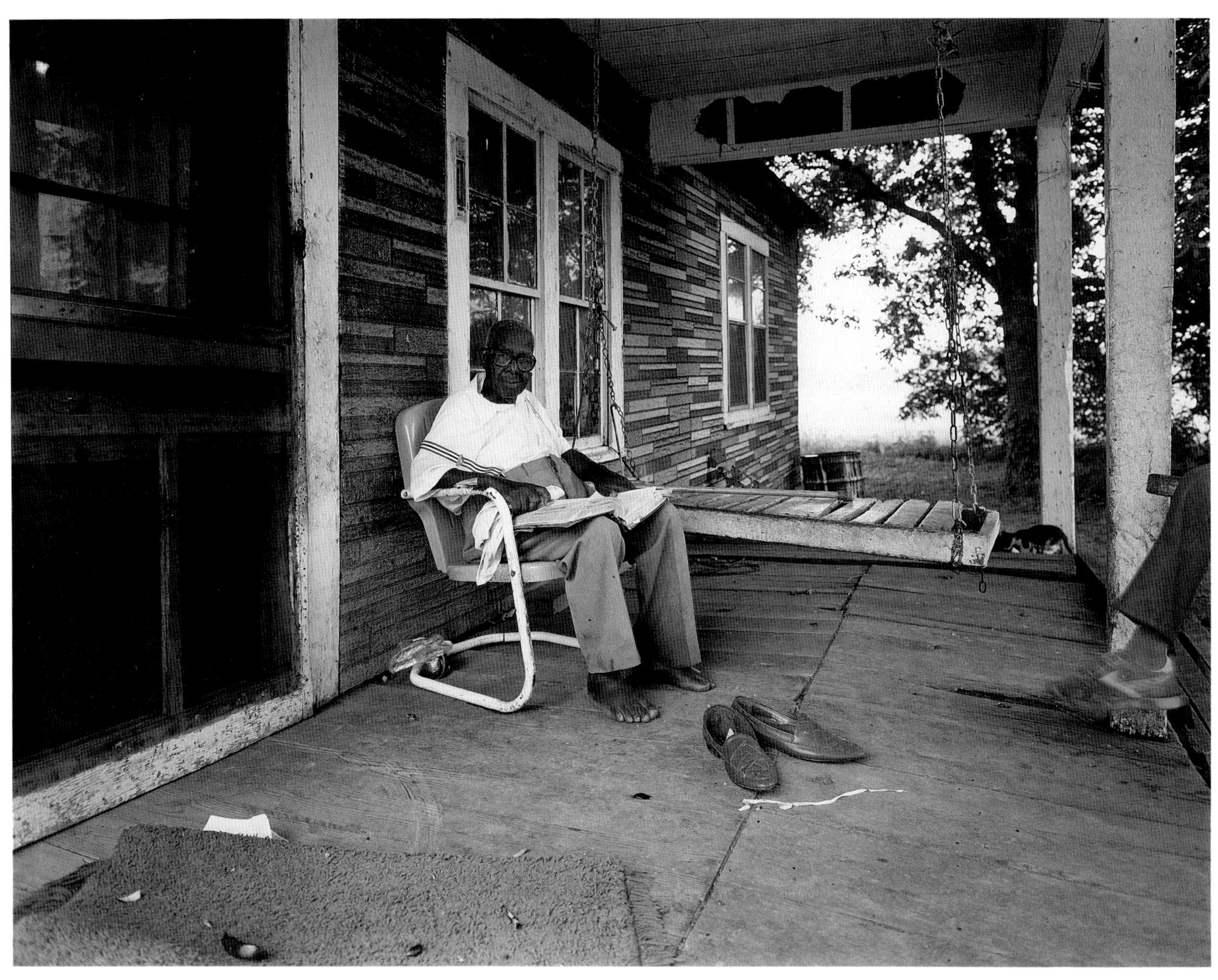

Reverend Tom Bronner at home,
Gunnison, 1989

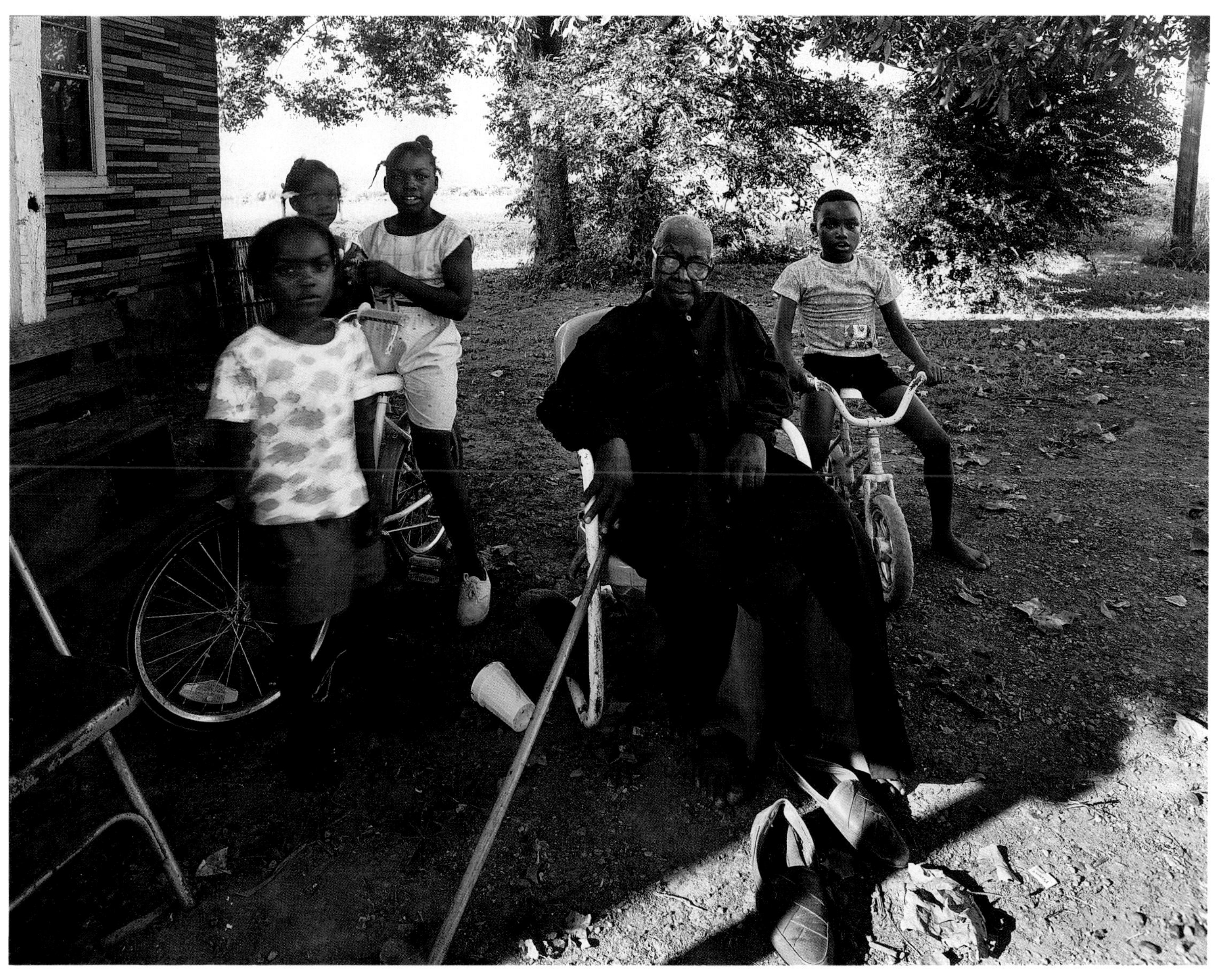

Reverend Tom Bronner with neighborhood children, Gunnison, 1989

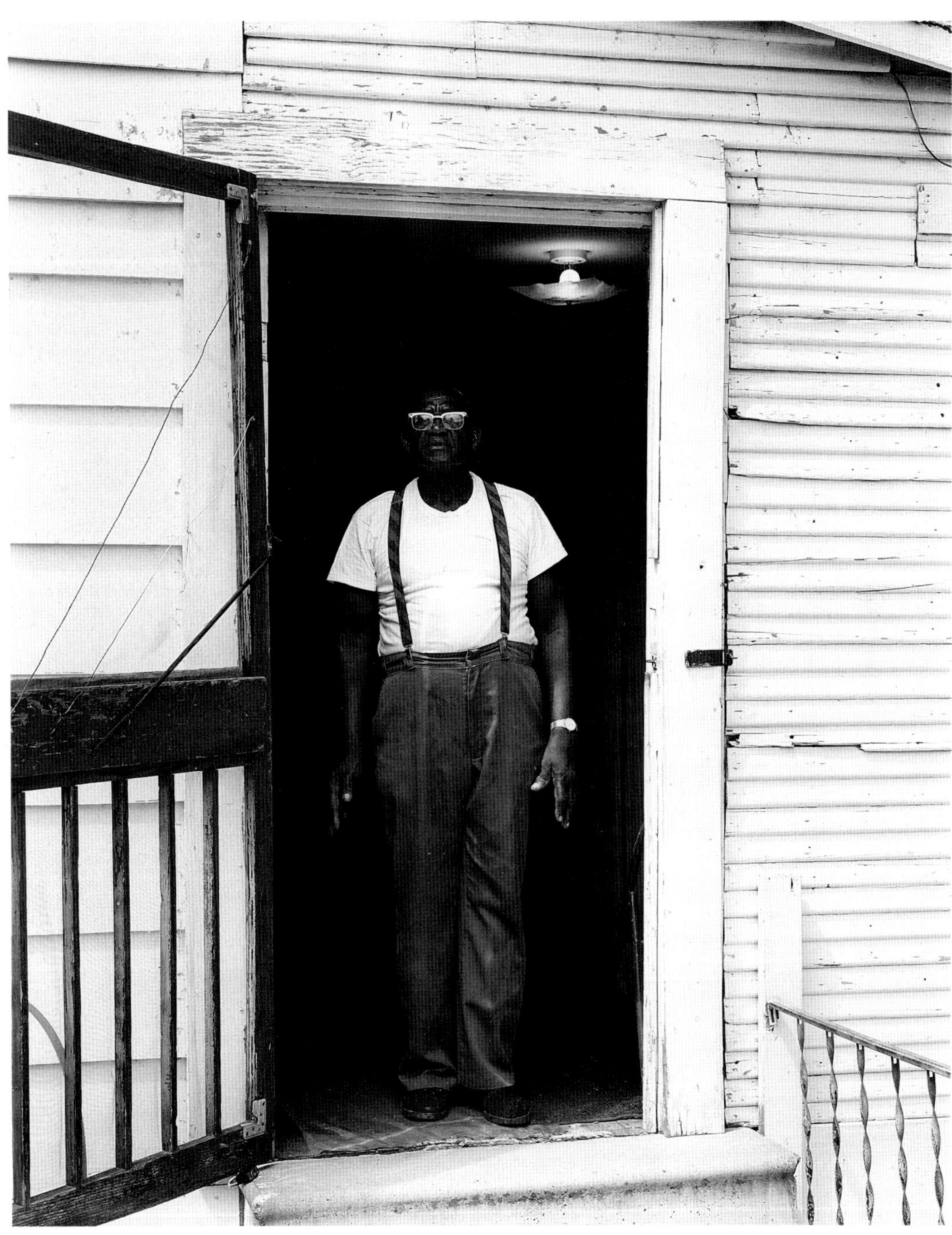

Reverend Brooks Tobe, Little Ebenezer Baptist Church, Rosedale, 1989

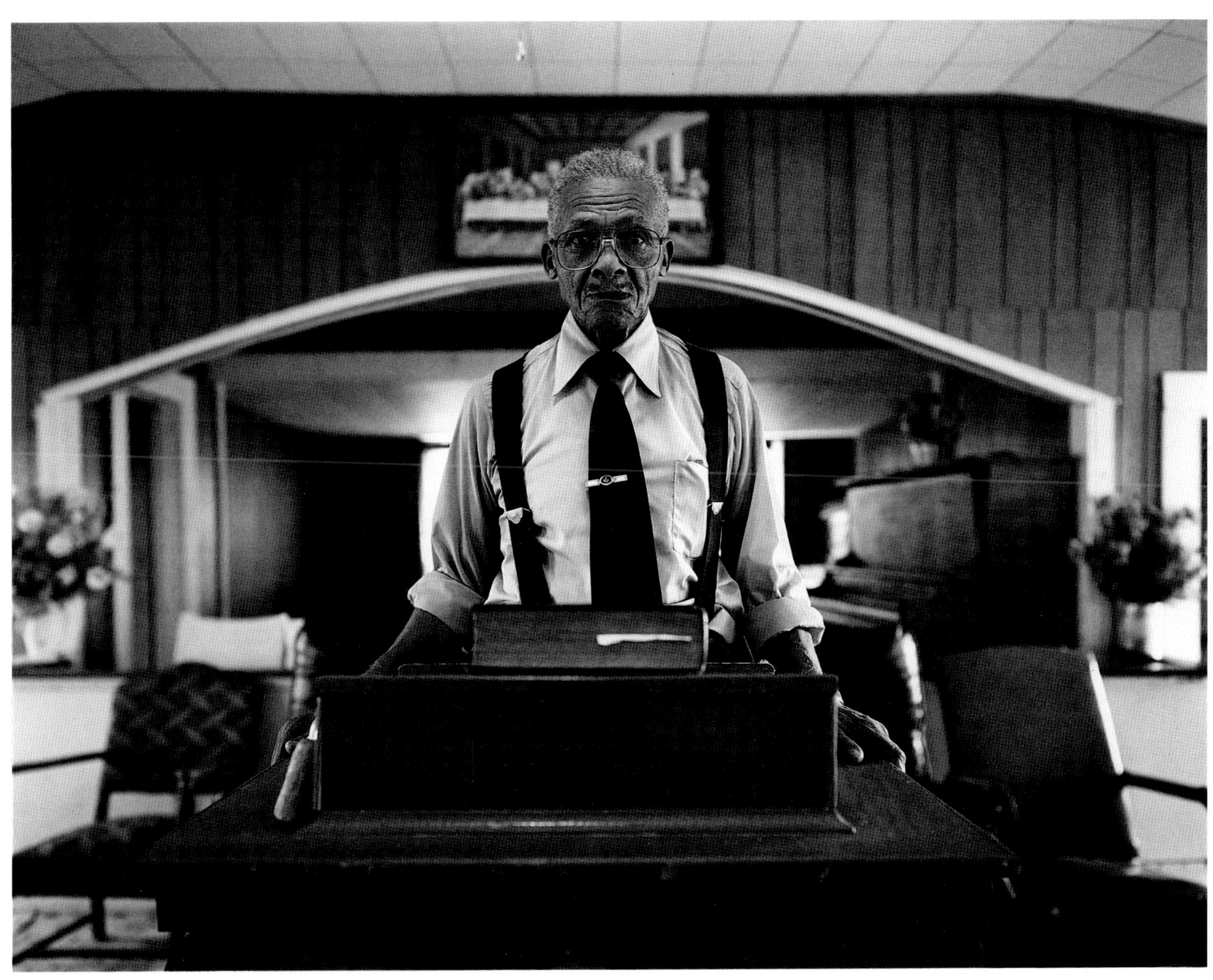

Reverend E. B. Brown, Mt. Pleasant M. B. Church, Beulah, 1989

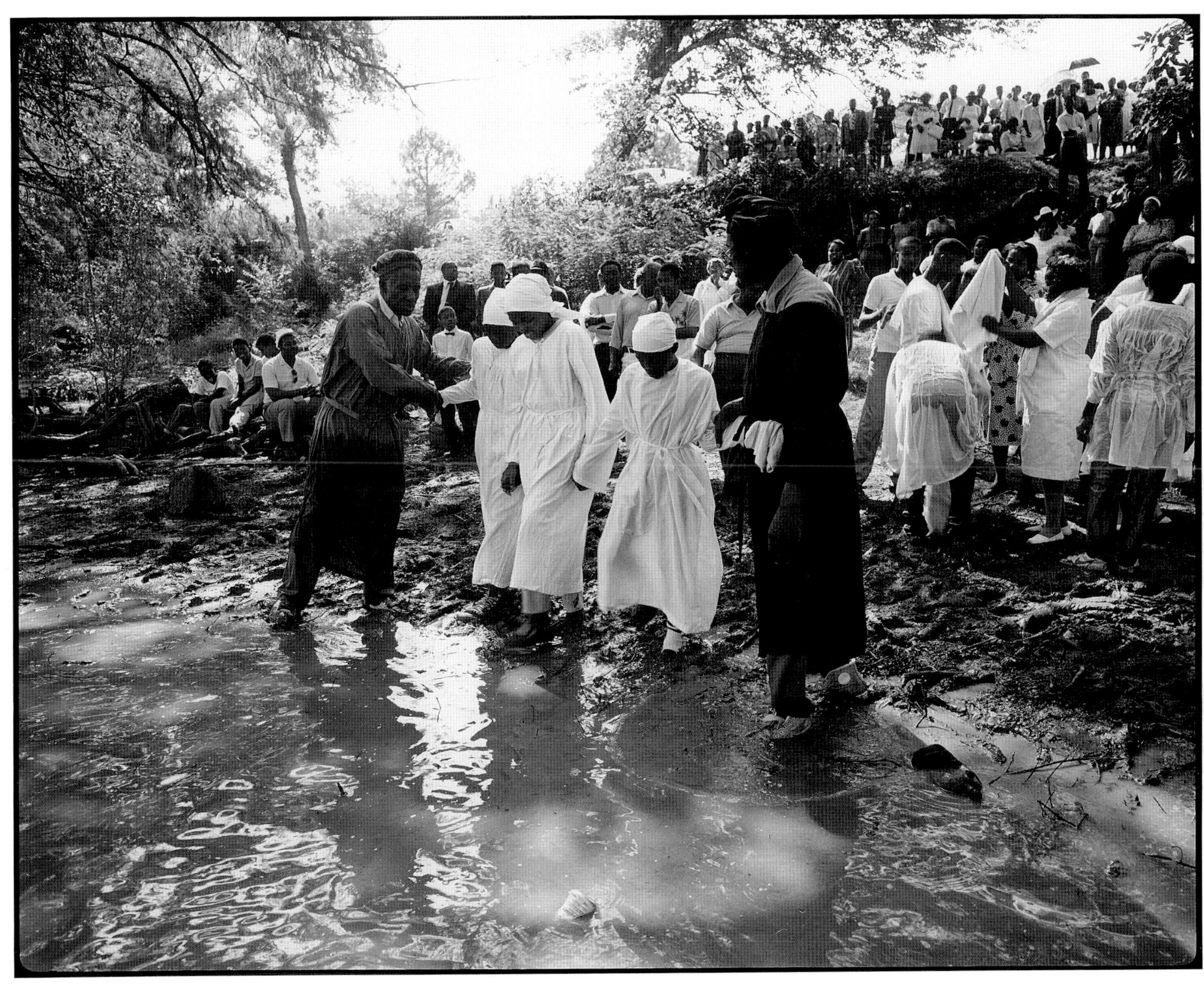

Baptism, Moon Lake, 1990

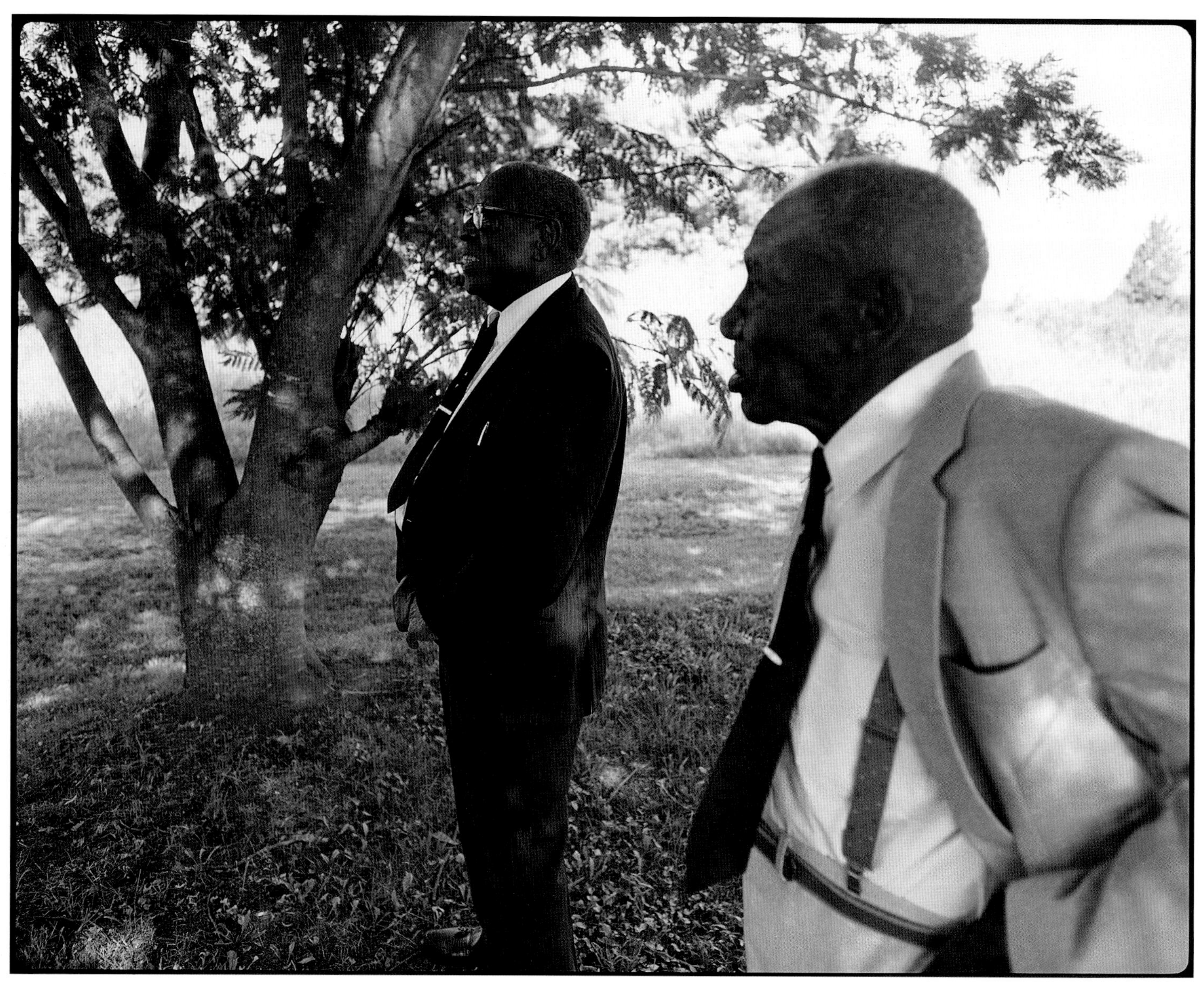

Baptism, Jerusalem M. B. Church,
Mound Bayou, 1989

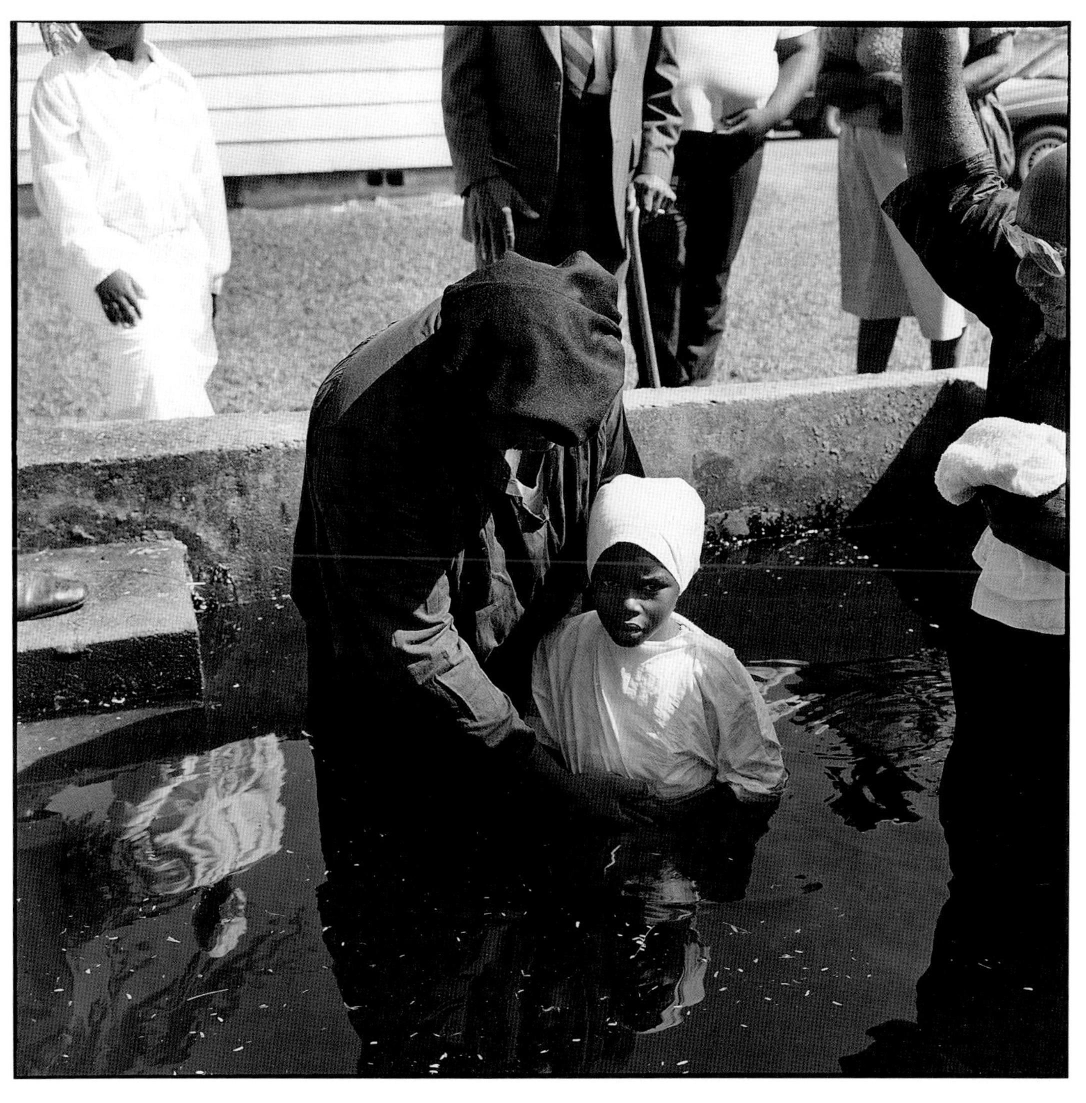

Baptism, Jerusalem M. B. Church,
Mound Bayou, 1989

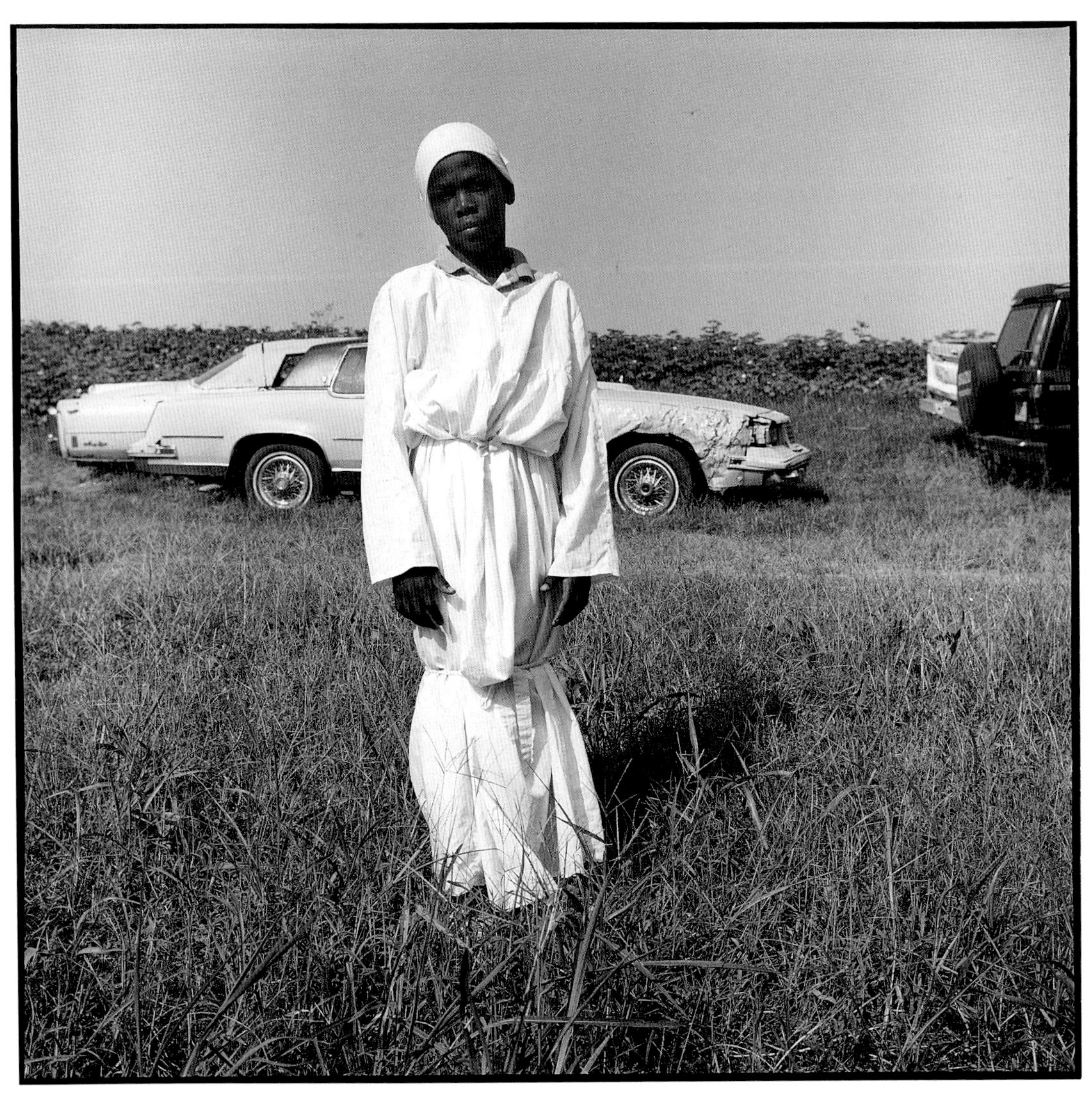

Candidate for baptism, fourth week in August, Perthshire, 1989

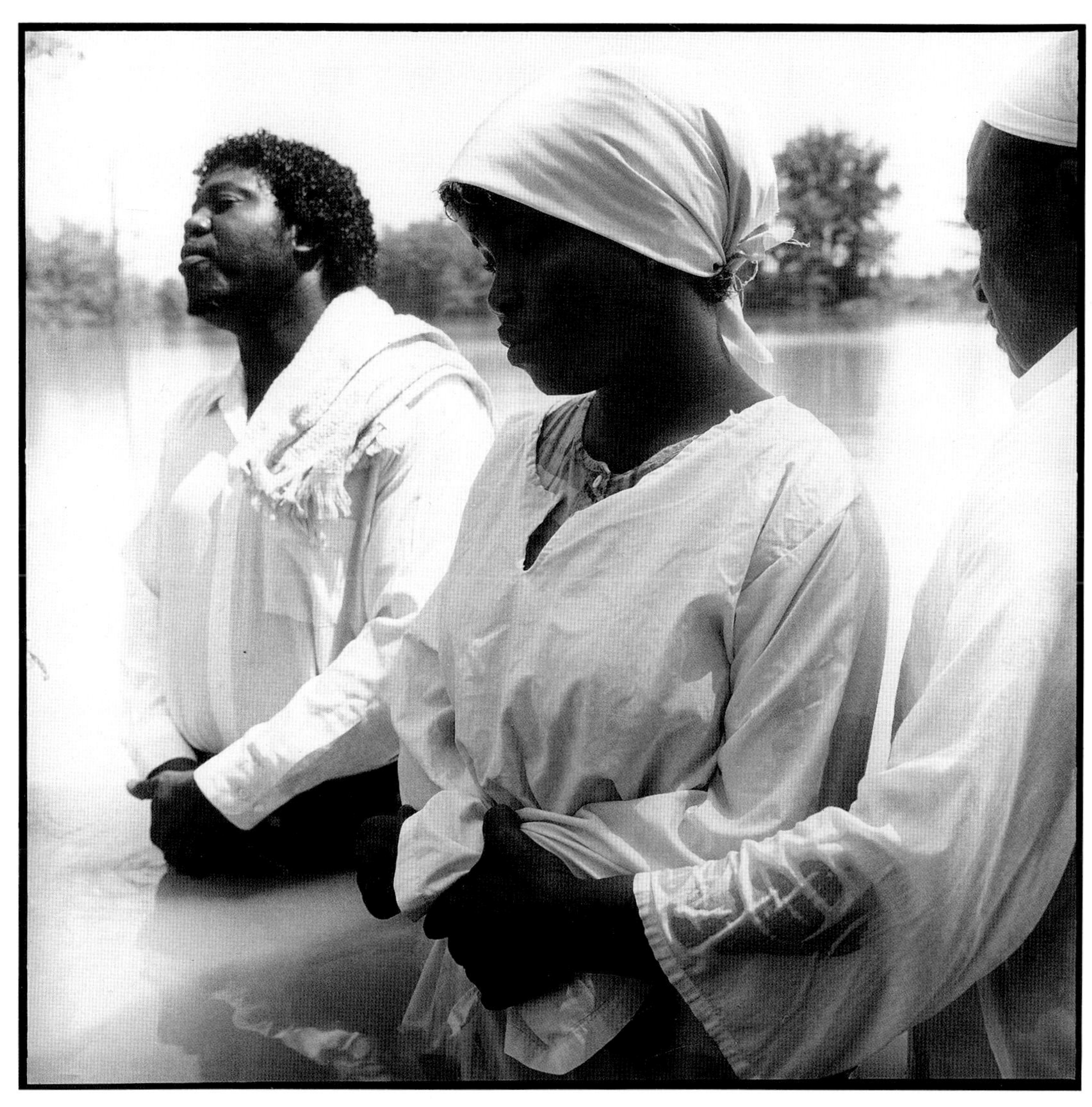

Baptism of Cheronda Brown by Reverend Crabtree, Stamps Lake, 1990

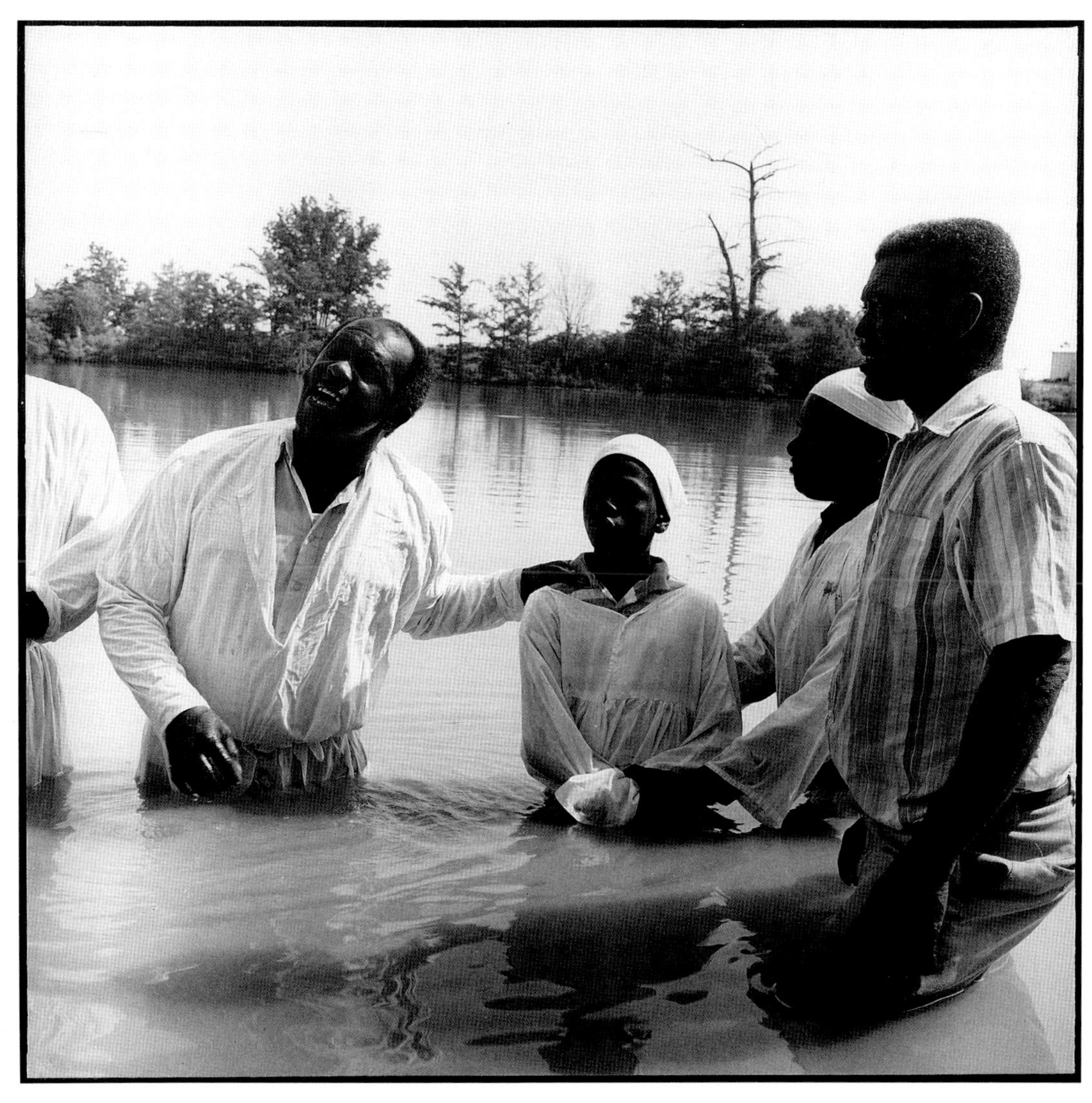

Baptism, Reverend Tom Meek,
Stamps Lake, 1989

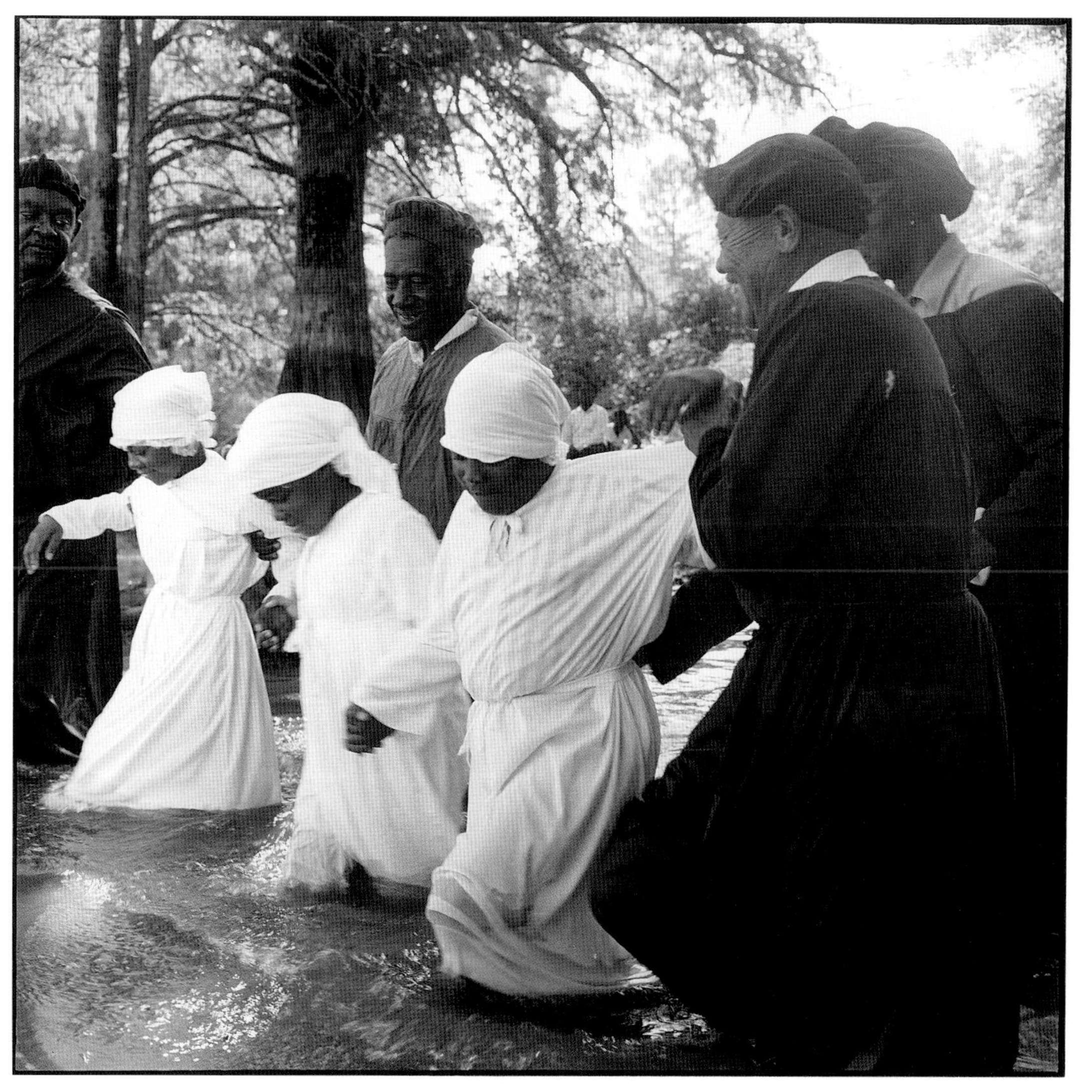

Moon Lake, 1990

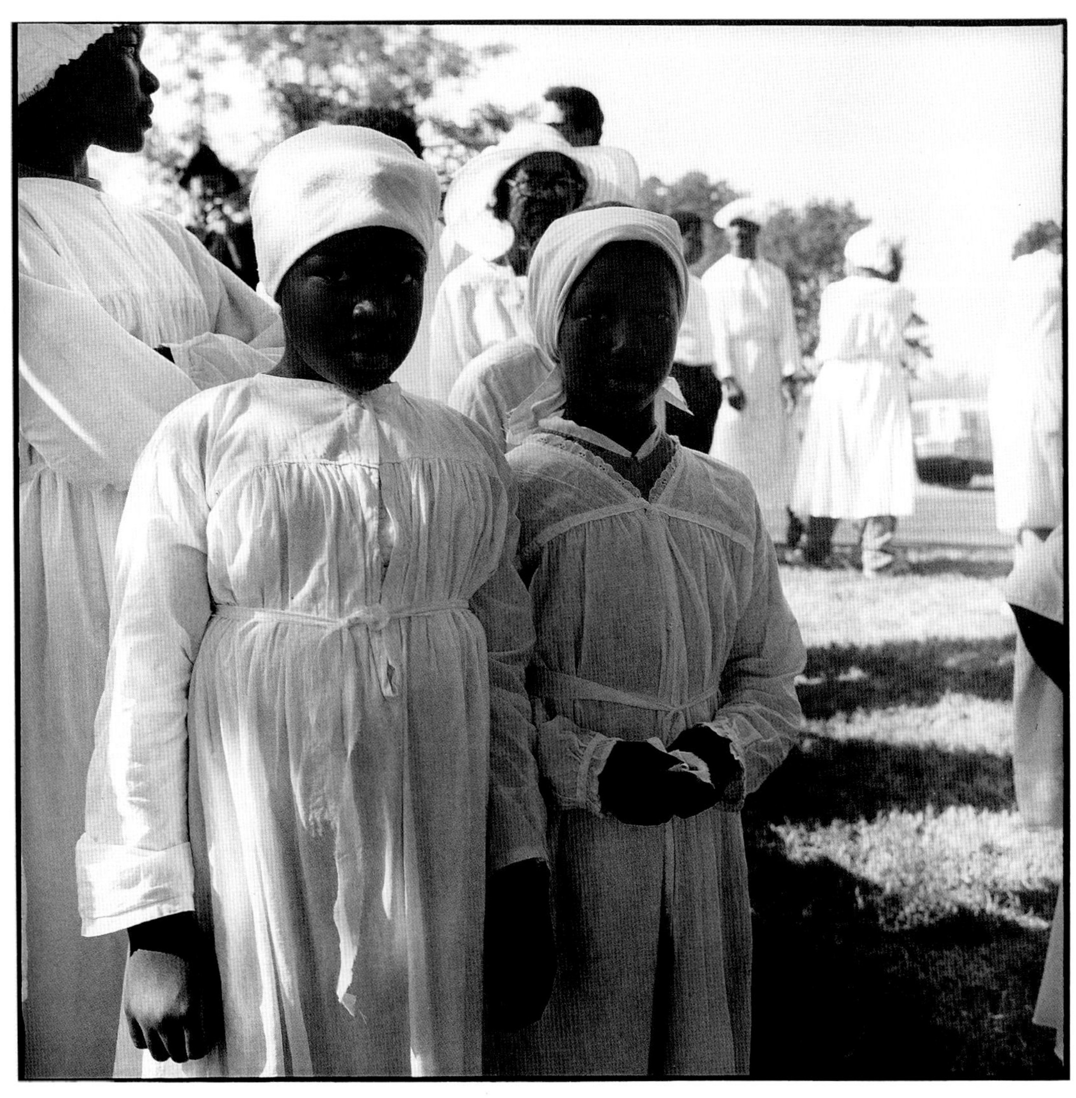

Juandra Griffin and Venita Murray,
Moon Lake, 1990

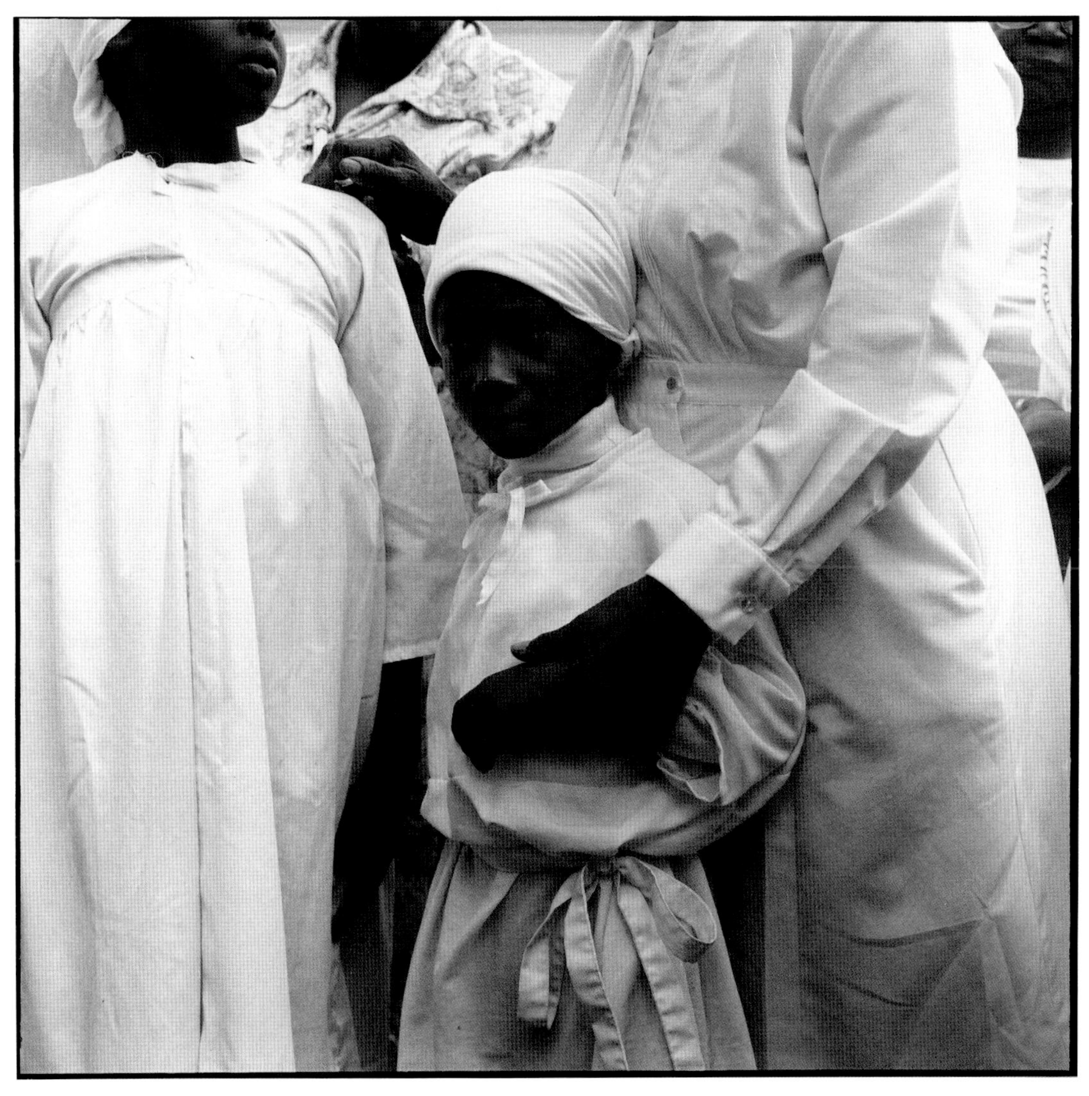

Candidate for baptism, Mound Bayou, 1990

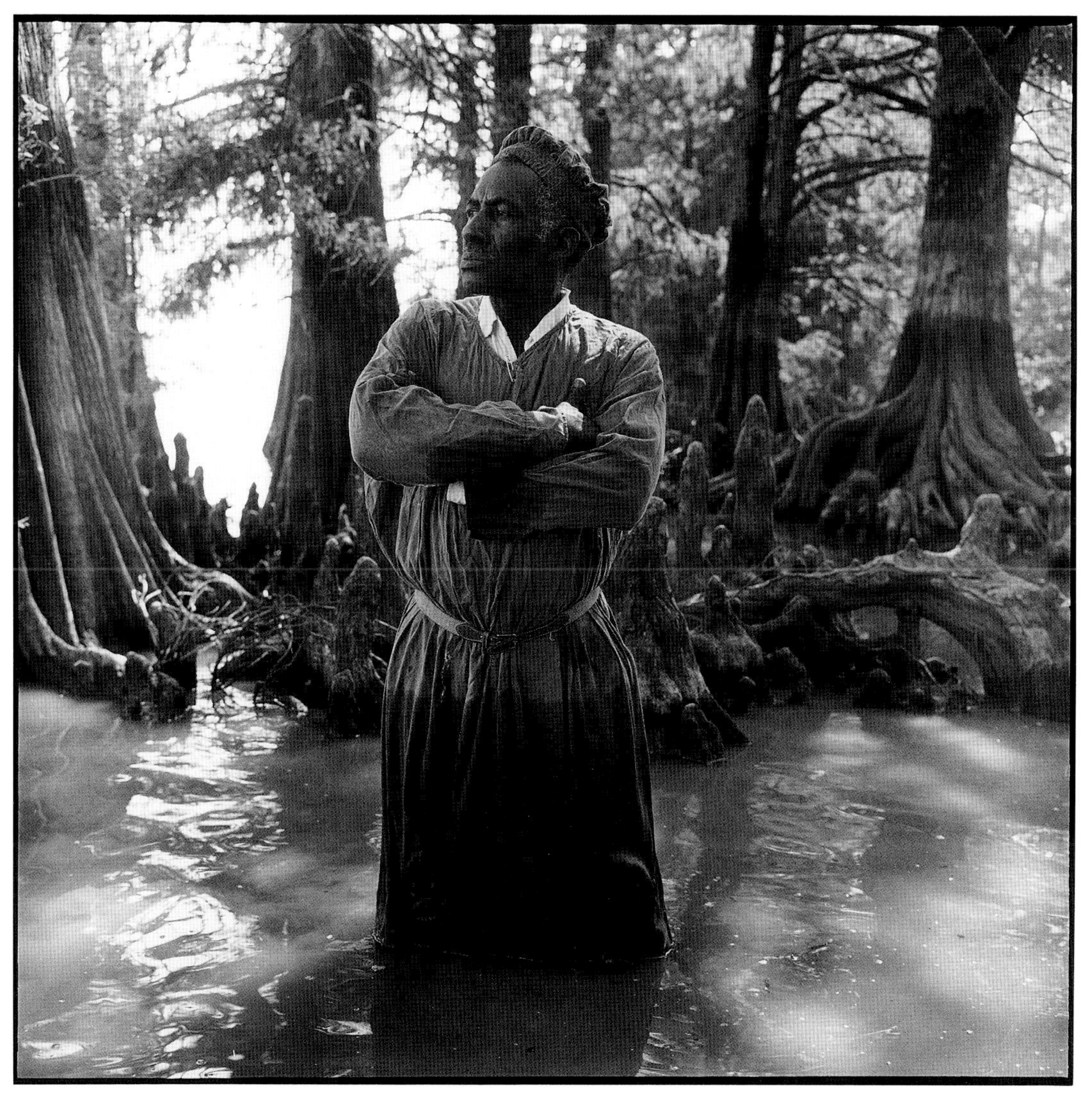

Deacon Fred Davis, Moon Lake, 1990

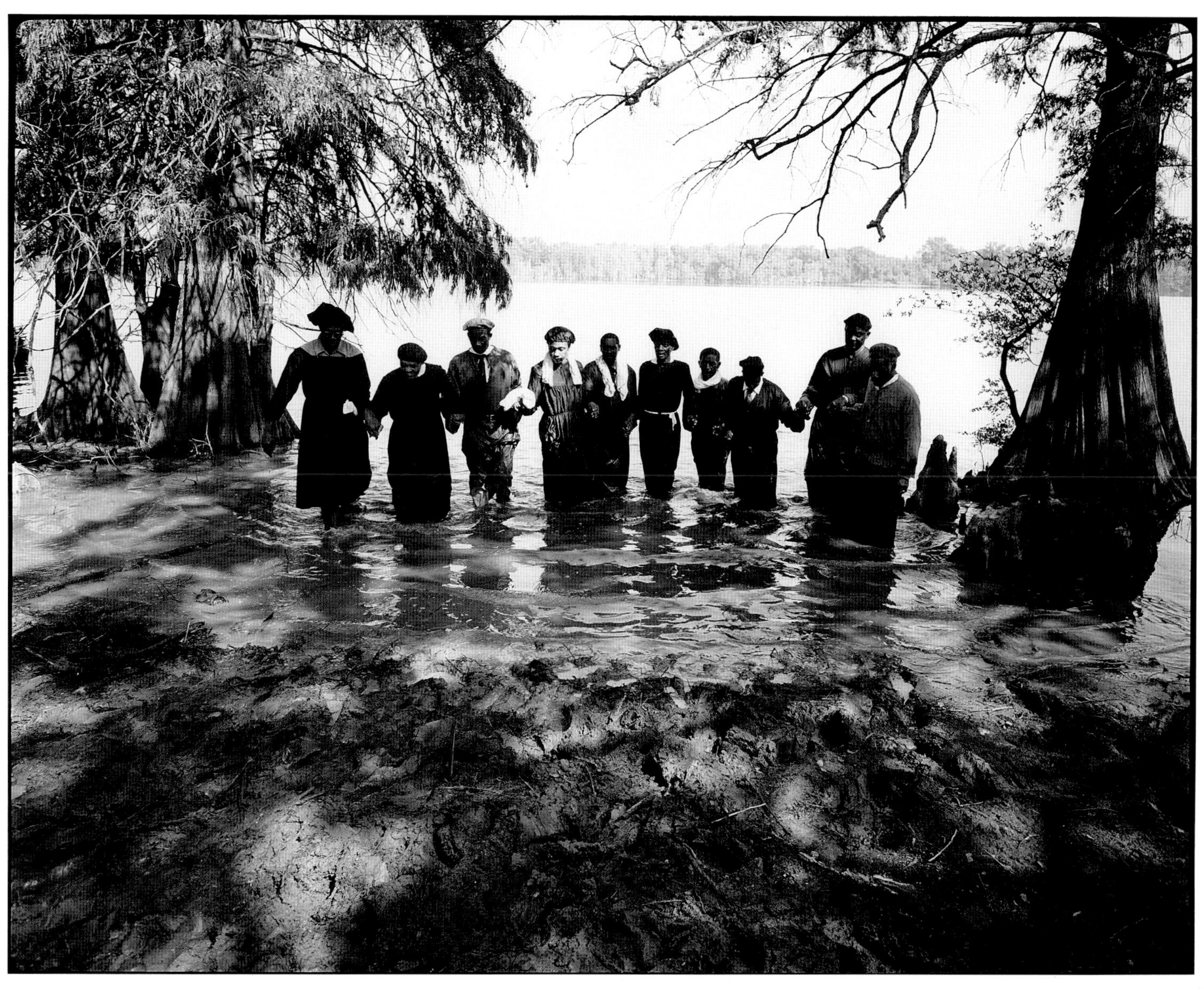

Prayer after baptism, Moon Lake, 1990

Acknowledgments

I find it difficult to acknowledge all who have contributed to this work. Jeff Todd Titon and Daniel W. Patterson first led me to understand my interest in sacred folk culture; my discussions with John McWilliams over the last five years were clearly helpful; the Susan B. Herron Visual Arts Fellowship from the Mississippi Arts Commission helped finance much of my photography in the Delta; and W. Frank McArthur and Delta State University believed in and supported this project from conception to delivery.

My greatest debt is to the members of the many communities throughout the Mississippi Delta who lent me their trust, respected my intentions, and opened the doors of their churches. In particular I want to acknowledge the assistance of Reverends Tom Bronner, Flem Bronner, P. R. Johnson, Brooks Tobe, E. B. Brown, E. T. Thrash, Herman Dennis, and Tom Meek. Georgia and Edward Moses of Bethlehem M. B. Church No. 2 in Shaw were generous and helpful. Special thanks to Mr. James Shelby for his graciousness. Others, far too numerous to mention, made my photography of African-American religious space possible through their willingness to cooperate.

I give special thanks to Charles Reagan Wilson for his foreword to this book and for his friendship and interest in my work. Thanks also to JoAnne Prichard and John Langston. Finally, heartfelt thanks go to Alexander, Julian, and Ruthie, who make my life a rich one and our home a kind of sacred space. Ruthie, to whom I dedicate this book, is a constant companion, patient supporter, and vital witness.